PRIORITIES, PLANNING AND PAPERWORK

Priorities, Planning and Paperwork

PETER BRIERLEY

All royalties from the sale of this book will be used for ongoing research on the church.

MARC

MARC Europe

British Church Growth Association

The section on 'The Perfect Secretary' in Chapter 6 is reprinted by
permission of the publisher from *The Time Trap* by R. Alec Mackenzie
© 1972 AMACOM, a division of the American Management Association. The extract from the poem 'Lord, I Have Time' from Michel
Quoist's *Prayers of Life* is reproduced with the permission of the
publishers, Gill and Macmillan, Dublin.

Front cover photo: Tony Stone photolibrary—London

Published jointly with MARC Europe, Vision Building,
4 Footscray Road, Eltham, London SE9 2TZ and
the British Church Growth Association, 3a Newnham Street,
Bedford MK40 2JR, who acknowledge the financial
assistance of the Drummond Trust, 3 Pitt Terrace, Stirling,
in the co-publication of this book.

MARC ISBN 1 85424 119 2
MARC Europe 0 947697 92 6
BCGA 0 948704 21 7

Printed in Great Britain for
MARC, an imprint of Monarch Publications Ltd
Owl Lodge, Langton Road, Speldhurst, Kent TN3 0NP by
Clays Ltd, St Ives plc
Typeset by Nuprint Ltd, Harpenden, Herts.

To my four children,
Stephen, Timothy, Kim and Michael,
who, though they know it not,
have helped me most to
learn how to value time

If you can dream and not make dreams your master,
If you think and not make thoughts your aim,
If you can meet with Triumph and Disaster,
And treat those two impostors just the same...

If you can fill the unforgiving minute,
With sixty seconds worth of distance run,
Yours is the earth and everything that's in it,
And what is more, you'll be a man, my son.

From 'If' by Rudyard Kipling

ACKNOWLEDGEMENTS

Time management is an art greatly aided by watching many practitioners at work. The essence of this book comes from the MARC Europe seminar 'The Effective Use of Time' and the handout which goes with it. Much of the material presented in Britain has been based on the handbook by Ed Dayton and Ted Engstrom on the equivalent American seminar, *Managing Your Time*. The British version has been rewritten by Bryn Hughes, the Director of Training at MARC Europe, helped by suggestions from Dr David Cormack, an Associate Director of Training. I am extremely grateful to each of these, who have laid a firm foundation on a key subject.

I am grateful too for my colleagues in MARC Europe who have helped me to practise what I preach. Especial thanks are due to Dee Frankling for her patient typing and retyping of the manuscript and to Suzanne Wardall for holding the fort while these pages were penned. My very warm appreciation goes to Valerie Passmore for her superb editing, and to Tony Collins, the publisher, for his constant encouragement, and to David Dryer, David Longley and Bryn Hughes for reading an early version of the manuscript and making most helpful comments.

CONTENTS

LIST OF DIAGRAMS

PSALM 23 FOR BUSY PEOPLE

The Lord is my pace-setter, I shall not rush,
He makes me stop and rest for quiet intervals,
He provides me with images of stillness,
     which restore my serenity.
He leads me in the ways of effectiveness
     through calmness of mind,
     and his guidance is peace.
Even though I have a great many things to accomplish each day
     I will not fret for his presence is here,
His timelessness, his all-importance will keep me in balance.
He prepares refreshment and renewal in the midst of my activity
     by anointing my mind with his oils of tranquillity,
My cup of joyous energy overflows.
Surely harmony and effectiveness shall be the fruit of my hours
     for I shall walk at the pace of my Lord,
     and dwell in his house for ever.

I

I DON'T HAVE ANY SPARE TIME

Goals and how to choose them

The scholar and writer C.S. Lewis is reputed to have once said, 'Christians often seem to have a lot of time; you may wonder where it comes from.' Many Christian people, church leaders or lay, would disagree! For many in today's world of constant communication, heightened expectations and activity-filled lives, a lot of time is what they do not have; in fact quite the reverse applies.

Have you noticed the type of person who may quietly take you aside? 'You're doing too much.' 'You're too busy.' 'Your diary is too full.' Without exception, kind friends who want to help are the busiest people we meet—those who are doing too much, who themselves are too busy and whose diaries are over-committed. At heart, the issue is not so much how busy you are, but why you are busy. The bee is praised. The mosquito is swatted.[1]

This book is for those who want to find more time to do the things that matter, who wish to plan more efficiently, and who desire to cope with the mountain of trivia which can so easily bury the essential. In short, it shows how to use time, how to save time, and how to share time.

Time

Time and tide alike may wait for no man, but they are two very different things.

The calling of time

There are different ways in which we can look at the time we have.

As a microcosm of life. J.B. Phillips translates Ephesians 5:15,16 particularly compellingly:

> Live life, then, with a due sense of responsibility, not as men who do not know the meaning and purpose of life but as those who do. Make the best use of your time, despite all the difficulties of these days.

In these verses Paul links the daily use of our time to the context of how we wish to live our whole lives. How we spend today partly reflects how we wish to spend our whole life.

As a line, not a circle. Time comes only once. Despite clocks having a circular face, with the implication that time keeps going round and round, time is actually a straight line; it never repeats itself. Exactly the same opportunity never recurs. Our calendar repeats itself each year, reflecting the earth's annual voyage around the sun, but we will not have the same chances next year to make up for those we failed to take this year. Time is linear, not circular. 'Every second that passes flies off into space and is gone.'[2]

Time is seen by Western standards not African ones for the large majority of people who read this book. Those who have lived in Africa, or even briefly visited that continent, know that Africans look at time quite differently. Said one: 'Westerners have the ideas, Africans have the time.' An African's sense of time is not dominated by the clock, or the radio pips, or Big Ben, or the nine o'clock news. But his time keeping is equally reliable. The Komos in Zaire, for example, call four o'clock in the morning 'Osa a kaka', or the time the cock crows; eight o'clock 'Beeka a mani', when the sun begins its ascent, and eleven 'Sanga a nkai', when the medicine man dances his incantations. This African ease with the passing of time is occasionally sensed in the West: a travel brochure for Ireland, for example, with the subheading 'Where all the time in the world isn't enough', captures the Irish proverb, 'When God made time, he made plenty of it.' It is not how we apportion time but how we use it that counts.

The characteristics of time

What, then, is time like? It may be worth pausing to note some basic characteristics. It is:

Inelastic. It cannot be stretched or compressed. We cannot make this precious minute two precious minutes. The most beautiful sunset lasts no longer than the more usual ones. While it may seem that a twenty-minute sermon lasts an hour, in reality the same clock times both listener and preacher. Elizabeth I's last words are reputed to be, 'All my possessions for a moment of time.' The same time is given to each of us and we are accountable for how we use it.

Expensive. One of the trends of the 1990s is 'economism', where everything is deemed to have a price—not just products and services but values too. Increasingly we are equating time with money. Anyone who has had to pay a taxi driver for waiting knows this. Some people who are unable to give money for a cause are willing to give their time to help. Conversely, others unable to give their time, give money.

Irreversible. Time cannot go backwards; we cannot have a replay· what we did not do yesterday was not done. As a sign in one vicarage said, 'Today is the tomorrow you worried over yesterday, and all is well.'

Irreplaceable. 'Do not squander time,' said the American statesman Benjamin Franklin, 'for that is the stuff life is made of.' However difficult the interview, awkward the letter, unpleasant the task, all have to be done, and we should not waste time in delaying them. The big and the small have to be fitted in. Whoever said little things should not bother you has not tried going to sleep with a mosquito buzzing round![3] You can do only one day's work today; why not do today's?

The conquest of time

As surgeons operate on a patient they are fighting for time. So much has to be done in a limited period. We may not be surgeons, but in our work, Christian or secular, how we cope with the battle of time is critical. The management lecturer, David Cormack, illustrates this with the analogy of a boxing ring in *Seconds Away*, his book on time management.[4] (The American edition is called *Fighting for Time*.)

If there is one battle people must win with themselves it is this. We all have 168 hours in the week, and 52 weeks in every year. The Australian Baptist minister, Rowland Croucher, in one of his 'Stress and Spirituality' seminars, speaking on the stress time pressure can cause, said, 'You have time to do everything God wants you to do. If you haven't enough time you are doing something God does not want you to do.'[5] That may be true, but it may also be that you are not organising yourself as efficiently as you might. A proverb says, 'Lose an hour in the morning, and you'll be all day hunting for it.' How may this be addressed, so that, as the priest Michel Quoist delightfully phrases it in his prayer, our time may be made a rich wine?

> Lord, I have time,
> I have plenty of time,
> All the time that you give me,
> The years of my life,
> The days of my years,
> The hours of my days,
> They are all mine.
> Mine to fill, quietly, calmly,
> But to fill completely, up to the brim,
> To offer them to you, that of their insipid water
> You may make a rich wine such as you made once in Cana
> of Galilee.

Visions

Lewis Carroll's Cheshire Cat got it right in his conversation with Alice:

'Would you tell me, please, which way I ought to go from here?' asked Alice.

'That depends a good deal on where you want to get to,' said the Cat.

'I don't much care where...' said Alice.

'Then it doesn't matter which way you go,' replied the Cat.

'If you don't know where you're going, you'll probably end up somewhere else,' is how Dr Lawrence Peter puts the same point. What do you wish to achieve? What is your vision for your life? What do you want to become? When Edward Heath was at grammar school, he was asked, 'Would you like to be Prime Minister?' He replied, 'I intend to be.' And he was!

Helmut Schmidt, the former West German Chancellor, one of the few world leaders to whom the Japanese listen carefully, candidly told those at a Tokyo seminar that 'Japan does not seem to know where it is going—there is no vision.'[6] It is not just countries which may have no vision. The well-known Bible verse, 'Where there is no vision, the people perish',[7] may be applied to others too: where there is no vision the churches perish; where there is no vision the leaders perish; where there is no vision you and I perish.

What is your vision for your life? A good way of finding out is to write your own epitaph. What would you like carved on your tombstone under your name? Here are some life summaries from the Scriptures:[8]

Enoch walked with God[9]
Moses, whom the Lord knew face to face[10]
Saul and Jonathan, beloved and lovely![11]
Before him [Josiah] there was no king like him[12]
Jehoram...departed with no one's regret[13]
Abraham, my friend[14]
Antipas, my witness, my faithful one.[15]

Which of these would you wish to follow? Presumably not Jehoram! John Calvin once said, 'My heart I give you, Lord, eagerly and entirely.' Would that sum up your life? An accountant friend once told me, 'I want to be a solid person,' by which she meant a person of integrity, rock-likeness, sureness. She was by nature solidly built, and her life philosophy matched her physical frame.

Your vision, therefore, is crucial for your life, and that works down to the individual years and events and opportunities. How does this relate to your use of time? How you spend your time depends ultimately on what you wish to do. What you decide to do needs to be consequent on what you wish to become as a person, or achieve as an individual or team.

Not being able to decide on the future is a problem for many. The American sociologist, Tony Campolo, in a videoed sermon, 'It's Friday but Sunday's coming', said the most important part of the gospel is not where you have come from but where you are going. That is not decided by your parents, or your spouse, but by Jesus Christ. We therefore need to look to Him in determining what our long-term plans might be.

This theme is worked out in more detail in the book *Vision Building*,[16] and the link between vision and purpose and goals is shown in the following diagram:

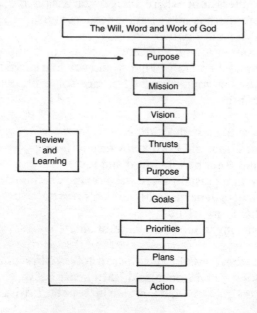

The *Will, Word and Work of God* reflects the overall sovereignty of God in making us as we are, putting us where we are now, and giving us opportunities to learn, to do and to follow. He is also the Creator of His church, the sender of His Spirit, and the ultimate Authority in the universe.

Note that there are two boxes labelled *purpose*. The first essentially relates to the basic foundation articles of the church or organisation. It may be enshrined in the memoranda of association, principles and practice, rules for members or legal documents setting out the reasons for the existence of a church or organisation.

Mission relates more to churches and organisations than to individuals. A clear mission statement is imperative. How we may get our *vision* is described at some length in the book *Vision Building*, and has been summarised by David Cormack as suggesting a vision must be:

V – ital
I – nspiring
S – imple
I – ntegrating
O – wned
N – ow

This vision describes where you want your organisation to be. It is right at the core of what you are about. *Thrusts* are the key initiatives which have to be taken in the fulfilment of our vision. For example, one of the six thrusts of World Vision is 'Strengthening Christian leadership'. The second *purpose* box relates much more to the outworking of these thrusts, and explains in more detail what these may be.

The remaining boxes relate to the components of this book: *goals* (this chapter), *priorities* (second chapter), *plans* (third and fourth chapters) and *action* (final chapters).

The immediate context of our goals and priorities, therefore, is the vision that we have for ourselves and for our church, organisation, job, responsibility or whatever and the thrusts by which it will be worked out. The creating of a vision is not easy, however, and may take some time. Nor is it necessarily fixed for ever, so some way of regularly reviewing your progress towards it is essential.

Purposes

In one way footballers have it easy. Their basic purpose is to win the game and ultimately the Cup. They do this by scoring goals. If a player kicks the ball but fails to see where it goes, the crowd's cheers will soon tell him whether or not he has scored a goal.

Christian organisations and churches are different because ultimately they desire a good harvest, and the harvest is not always easily defined, nor is the harvest field always exactly identified. A ripening field of wheat is nowhere as specific as a football net fifty yards away. A field and a net are similar in that both are motivational. They are also different, and the difference between a field and a net portrays the difference between a purpose and a goal. Christian organisations and churches have a higher allegiance than the basic purpose of the organisation—they relate to the Will, Word and Work of God. They are different because the individuals in the church or organisation share in this common allegiance to the 'God who is there'. This should give them higher moral and ethical standards than in the secular world.[17]

Purpose statements

Purpose statements of the type relating to the top 'purpose' box in the diagram on page 22 answer the question 'Why?' Why are you doing this? Why do you wish to become that? Here are two examples from *Vision Building*:

> The Mother's Union is 'specially concerned with all that strengthens and preserves marriage and Christian family life.'
> St Agnes Roman Catholic Church, Gateshead, 'serves the spiritual needs of the parishioners of Crawcrook and surrounding areas.'

Defining 'purpose' (the higher box in the diagram) is good in order to put everything in context. It is to that purpose that our vision relates. This book, however, is concerned with how we work out our time, reflected through our goals and priorities and plans, and we will not, therefore, dwell longer on the 'thrusts' box or above. Those who want a fuller explanation are invited to read *Vision Building*.

The lower 'purpose' box tends to answer the question 'What?' What are you doing to fulfil that thrust? What are you intending to become? Examples of such uses might be for:

A church	● To build up the membership in the knowledge of Christ
	● To strengthen our witness in our parish
	● To guide those with difficulties in their personal life
An individual	● To become a better manager
	● To be an effective parent
	● To develop a better understanding of Christian mission.

Such purposes may relate to our *aim*. 'My aim is to get a good degree,' an individual may say; 'Our aim is to reach our whole town,' a church might state. Our purpose may relate to our *mission*. The word is used in this way frequently by Christian organisations. 'Our mission is to win the lost.' A Christian editor may say, 'My mission is to publish quality books.' Our purpose may relate to our *objectives*. The word is often used in this sense by the military: 'Our objective is to take that hill.' It is used by many charitable organisations too in such words as 'to care for the needy'. An individual researcher may say, 'My objective is to develop my interpretation ability.'

Goal statements

But what actually are goals? It may be helpful to describe goals in a personal way. What do they mean to you as an individual?

Goals answer the question 'How?' How am I going to accomplish this? How does the church reckon on doing that? How will the organisation fulfil that promise?

Such goals may be phrased in relation to specific *objectives* or *targets*. 'My goal this year is to master the rudiments of Greek,' a student might say; 'Our goal this year is to raise £100,000,' a charity might consider. Such goal statements might focus more on the *task*. 'I will sweep the leaves off our back lawn every week in the autumn,' a gardener might think. 'We will deliver our magazine three times to every house in our parish this year,' a minister might propose. Such statements might relate more to the *steps* that have to be taken. 'Our aim in Phase 1 is to lay good foundations before the winter sets in,' an architect might declare. My youngest son is reading for a degree in Anglo-Saxon at Cambridge: 'I must take history for A-level,' he had said two years before.

The difference between purposes and goals

We are using the words 'purpose' and 'goal' quite specifically here. You may wish to use other words, and some books on time management do. The terms do not matter but the essential concepts of these two words must be maintained.

There is a crucial difference between them. The dividing line is one of measurement, thus:

Purpose	Not measurable
The Dividing Line is Measurement	
Goal	Measurable

Purposes are statements of intent; goals are explicit statements of action. Purposes state what we are going to do in general terms; goals state precisely how we reckon on achieving it. A purpose is something for which we ultimately hope, a desire, clear direction towards which we wish to move. A goal is a time-related standard identifying achievement. The differences between them may be set out as follows, with examples as an individual might state:

Purposes		Goals	
Description	Example	Description	Example
General	I wish to be an effective teacher.	Specific	I will spend six hours a week in preparation.
Not measurable	I want to know my Bible better.	Measurable	I will read four chapters a day for the next year.
Universal	We should reach others.	Achievable	I will speak to John Smith this week about Christ.
Wishful thinking	I need to know more about management.	Realistic	I will read one chapter of a book on management every day for a month.
Periodic	We should become more thrifty.	Timed	I will write down our exact income and expenditure every week.

The goal column answers the question of the purpose 'How am I going to do this?', the purpose column the goal question 'What am I doing this for?'

There is so much muddled thinking in this area, with statements of one kind being made mistakenly as the other. To ensure you understand what a purpose is, stop for a moment and choose, say, three of the following lines to write an appropriate purpose statement.

One purpose of my

Job is: _____

Church is: _____

Home is: _____

Leisure is: _____

Career is: _____

Organisation is: _____

Reading is: _____

Now spend a few minutes looking at the following state-ments. (If you are a minister or church worker take A; if you are a lay person take B. Which of these statements are purposes and which goals?

A: Ministers   Purpose or
                                                   goal?

1 Visit three nearby families who don't go to
   church next week.   _____

2 See my church grow week by week.   _____

3 Prepare next two sermons with at least
   twenty-four hours to spare.   _____

4 Preach shorter sermons.   _____

5 Work on fewer committees.   _____

6 Take a trip to the Holy Land the year after next. _____

7 Spend an extra fifteen minutes in prayer every
   day for six weeks starting on the first day of
   next month.   _____

8 Move to a larger church.   _____

9 Spend more time with my family.   _____

10 Read one book on leadership by the end of
   next month.   _____

(Please note that item 4, 'preaching shorter sermons', should not be labelled 'wishful thinking'!)

B: Lay People   Purpose or
                                                   goal?

1 Read a book each week for the next month.   _____

2 Be a more gracious person.   _____

3 Read the Bible more often.   _____

4 Learn to sail by the end of the summer.   _____

5 Play more with my children.   _____

6 Attend the Christian convention being held
   next Easter.   _____

7 Give a regular amount to the church each
   week for the next month.   _____

8 Move to a better home.   _____

9 Increase my income.   _____

10 Thank at least one person a day for the whole
    of the next two months.   _____

You should have five purposes and five goals from either list.

Goals

If our purposes are important, our goals are even more so. Goals help you to think ahead. I do not agree with everything Robert Schuller, pastor of the Los Angeles Crystal Cathedral, writes, but I am sure he is right when he says, 'When you set no goals for growth, you set your goals for no growth.'[18] It is critical to have goals.

Is goal setting unspiritual?

Should we not rely on the Holy Spirit? Yes, we should, but He is the Spirit who leads us, guides us into the truth, and there is no reason to believe that He should not help us with setting our goals a year ahead of fulfilment as well as in accomplishing them. Goal setting can strengthen our faith as we see prayer answered. Goals are for the congregation, as their fulfilment is a source of encouragement. (The congregation, therefore, should help to set them.) How thankful Paul was when the various Asian churches contributed to the needs of the Jerusalem churches. Sometimes goals can be too numerous or too extravagant. Have just a few goals for yourself or your church—say a maximum of five. Then the reality of the situation can be seen and the outcome can be prayed over as the year proceeds.

One London church makes a goal of its mission budget each year. It was £37,000 in 1990. Half way through the year only

£13,000 had been raised. They reviewed the situation. People were asked to pray; the situation was explained in detail; the consequences of non-fulfilment outlined. The result was that the full £37,000 was received. Had the figures either not been announced publicly or not mentioned during the year, almost certainly the final total would have been much less. Far from being unspiritual, goal setting can stimulate faith, prayer and general good works.

Individuals need to be allowed to work out their own goals, rather than being told what they should be by their superior or peers. A superior may need to agree goals, but the initiative for identifying them should lie with the individual concerned. In this way motivation is retained, as are relevance and realism.

How does this work in a church? Should the minister not set goals for the Sunday school, say? No; he should ask the Sunday school superintendent or youth leader for his/her goals over the next year. The minister can always discuss them with the leader and suggest they are lowered if felt to be unduly optimistic or increased if overpessimistic. Realistic goals are required. Responsibility is given with accountability and the twinning of these two is a powerful motivation. The saying 'My goals are good goals, your goals are bad goals' reflects this emphasis. I don't want to work on your goals, so in that sense, as far as I am concerned, they are 'bad goals', though doubtless good goals for you. My own goals I am happy to work on so they are 'good goals' for me, but they would be bad goals, unrealistic goals, inappropriate goals, for you.

Good goals

What are good goals? David Cormack, who has taken many MARC Europe seminars, suggests they should have the five characteristics given earlier which spell out the word SMART:

S –pecific
M –easurable
A –chievable
R –ealistic
T –imed

Goals which contain these five criteria are more easy to communicate. They identify what is significant, and help clarify who is expected to do what. People usually feel their relevance. They become personal and motivational. Poorly written goals are stated as a process or activity, ambiguous, never fully achievable, idealistic, theoretical, too brief or too long. How good are you in writing such goals? Write beside the purposes from the previous exercise goal statements which conform to these standards:

Purpose	*Goal*
See my church grow week by week.	_____
Preach shorter sermons.	_____
Work on fewer committees.	_____
Move to a larger church.	_____
Spend more time with my family.	_____
Be a more gracious person.	_____
Read the Bible more often.	_____
Play more with my children.	_____
Move to a better home.	_____
Increase my income.	_____

Another important facet of a good goal is that it is *reviewable*. If you have been unrealistic this year, be more sensible next year. Review the situation. This is vital. After 40 per cent of the time span for a goal, ask 'How are we doing?' If you have not accomplished your goal, hold a post-mortem, as my colleague, Bryn Hughes, says, to find out where something went wrong, so that you can correct it.

Goals are future events

Goals are like a photograph of the future—an image or picture of how it may be. Where might God want you to be in five years' time? What will you have accomplished in five years' time? What is the first step (the sub-goal) you need to take now to begin to make it happen?

Goals help you to *look forward*. They face your future, not your past. They are future events that can be accomplished.

Realism is their watchword. It would be foolish of me to think I could ever climb Everest, for instance: my physique, lack of training and of motivation would make setting such a goal pointless for me. But I am game for a twenty-mile sponsored walk. That is possible, and could easily be a goal for next year.

Goals are future events that you can *measure over time*, that is, there is a stated date by which your goal should have been achieved.

Goals are future events that can be *measured by performance*. You will be able to identify whether or not they have been achieved. At some time your goals will become *past* events, that is, history.

Goals are future events towards which we can *measure progress*, often in a series of steps, or sub-goals. The goal might need to be changed or modified by future circumstances. For instance, to raise £200,000 by the end of next year I need to have good publicity, names of people to approach, a clear statement of why the money is needed and who will be entrusted with its use. Each of these is a step to eventual realisation and could be expressed diagrammatically.

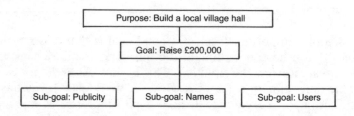

In this simple example publicity, potential donors and the users are subservient to knowing why the money is needed. Setting out goals in this way helps to focus on those especially vital elements or steps of a programme. If you found a person who was willing to give, say, £100,000, but in eighteen rather than twelve month's time, the goal changes to raising the other half, and the sub-goal *also* changes to raising money to match what has already been promised.

Setting out sub-goals in this way also identifies the responsibilities at different levels. The management trainer, Mark Silverside, calls such sub-goals 'objectives' or 'tasks' to aid this identification process.[19] This kind of diagram also differentiates goals as immediate, short-term, and longer-term or ultimate goals.

Goals are a response to a perceived need

They are, therefore, a challenge as one cannot be sure the need will be met. Goals which fulfil a need, however, are motivated.[20] What kinds of need are meant? The psychologist, Abraham Maslow, identified a five-level hierarchy of needs for the individual. The most basic need is to survive: to have enough food and air. Then we require safety and security. Assured of these we look for friendships and relationships, and after these seek value in the eyes of our associates. The highest need is that growth which comes from serving others. How may this system apply to the church?

The lowest level is simply that of *survival*. We need to have a core of church members, adequate finance, equipment and housing and transport for the church leader, and similar features in a church organisation. The things necessary to survive personally (food, shelter, clothing) are reflected in what is the minimum when you talk of 'my church'.

If the church or organisation is to thrive it needs to feel in *safety* without, for instance, fear of a merger with another parish, takeover by another group or inadequate cash flow. A warmth level comes from the fellowship. This assumes a model in the leader's mind of what he or she will feel comfortable with. Team members are highly motivated when they are asked to undertake tasks which enable them to be the kind of person they want to be.

Above safety lies *affiliation*, the ability to perform because one belongs. The second level of leadership should support the first; deacons or council should support their pastor, minister or leader. You seek then to give teaching to deepen that fellowship or to increase the call of discipleship and evangelistic concern. Affiliation also means continuing membership, a type of status. Thus leaders can give status to others because they can offer membership and the security that brings. This assumes that belonging to your church means something—that members are expected to be involved in some types of activity. Working with your organisation satisfies the employees because it enables them to do what they are wanting to do. They are in a position to achieve their own goals.

Esteem comes above affiliation, and may be reflected from the approval of your superintendent, bishop, chairman, district commander or trustees. Here there is an affirmation from the leadership level above you, giving you strength as a consequence. Few of us can exist as isolated individuals. Giving and receiving affirmation and approval is essential. Just as each member of your team wants to be wanted, so naturally you do too. There is a danger here, however, that wanting to be loved can inhibit setting certain goals if you fear that a relationship might be weakened as a consequence.

The highest step is *service*. Fulfilment comes from growth. Paul talks of having no more use for childish ways now that he is a man.[21] Little children often describe what they will do 'when I'm bigger'. Growth reaches its peak in adulthood, and desire for service is strongest then. It is at this level too that goal setting can be easier, as you have the security of all the other levels of need satisfied. Your desire is to achieve the full potential of your church, your organisation, your specialist ministry.[22]

Goals are a statement of faith

Stating a goal is no guarantee of its fulfilment. We can only believe it may happen. It is therefore a statement of faith.

Goals are based *both* on the knowledge of what God has already done *and* on what He has promised. David took on Goliath after his successful experience with both the lion and the bear. Jack Hayford, pastor of a large church in California, prays for his church's finance. Early in his ministry, when he was asking God for 'more money', he felt that he ought to pray more specifically but did not know how much to request. So he asked God to show him for how much he should pray. He felt the answer was $2,000 a month, but says quite candidly, 'I won't be offended if anyone accuses me of imagining the number.' After four months he records that without any special appeals the monthly income stood at $1,700. One day when he was praying he felt his usual request for $2,000 was not right and sensed a voice saying, 'Why haven't you asked the Father lately for a new amount?' He did and immediately felt he should increase his request to $3,000 a month. He would say this was not setting goals, simply asking questions of his Father. He entirely supports the importance of direction, strategy and planning, and is concerned that goal setting does not become a simple intellectual man-generated exercise, but rather that it reflects the leading of the Holy Spirit.[23] Walking by faith, as it is sometimes phrased, is no different from believing in God to fulfil the goals you have set as you have sought to express His will for your life, your church or your organisation.

The Scriptures encourage us *to act in a concerted way*—to share our goals, if you wish. It was four men together who wished to bring their paralysed friend to Jesus, and finding the crowd too thick to force a way through went upstairs and opened the roof. It was when Jesus saw *their* faith that he said to the man, 'My son, your sins are forgiven.'[24]

Likewise we are encouraged *to have a sense of limit* to our action. We are called to do something but not to do everything. Realism is essential. On at least one occasion Jesus gave explicit limiting instructions: 'Do not go among the Gentiles or enter any town of the Samaritans.'[25] Paul wrote that 'we... will confine our boasting to the field God has assigned for us, a field that reaches even to you.'[26] Their work and faith, in these instances, was to be limited to the groups in question. It was not that others were not important, or that they could not be reached at other times, but for this time it was to be just this area of activity.

The Bible also indicates *the importance of progression*. The verse in Acts 1:8 promising power when the Holy Spirit comes reflects the consequence of the witnessing of the early Christians, first to Jerusalem with its 100,000 normal population swollen to 250,000 on account of pilgrims attending the festival. Then they were to go to the 700,000 in Judea and Samaria. Finally they were to go to the rest of the 170 million people then alive—the ends of the earth. Moses too was told of the gradual victory that would be accomplished as the Israelites entered their Promised Land: 'The Lord your God will drive out those nations before you, little by little.'[27]

Progression is important, but it is also essential *to be specific when we pray*. One of many verses which underline this is Mark 11:24: 'Whatever you ask for in prayer, believe that you have received it, and it will be yours.' Brian Mills, who planted the prayer triplet movement, tells the story of the man who prayed for years that his neighbour would be converted, but to no avail. He realised he needed to be more specific and so prayed for an opportunity just to talk with his neighbour. That week found them both cleaning their cars at the same time, so a conversation was readily established. Then he prayed that he might have an opportunity to serve his neighbour, and the following week his neighbour's wife locked herself out of the house; could she borrow his ladder to get in through the bedroom window? Then he prayed he might be able to talk to his neighbour about his faith. When cutting the lawn the neighbour chatted over the fence and asked him where he and his family went every Sunday morning. Then he prayed that his neighbour might come to the church and, on being invited to the special harvest service, he gladly came. Then he prayed they might come again, and be converted. They did, and they were. How specific are you when you pray? What goals, as it were, do you set? Goals are simply a statement of our faith.

Writing goal statements

Some people find goal statements *difficult to write*. But the writing process frequently crystallises the thinking process and provides a crisper result on the one hand, and a sharable result on the other.

Goal statements should conform to the following criteria:

- Write one goal per sentence.
- State the final result (it must be measurable!)
- Give the time limit for achievement (it must be possible!)
- Define the standard/results expected.

However hard it may be—and it becomes much easier with practice—do persevere! There is nothing worse than two people working on conflicting goals simply because they never shared them; communicating goals is a thousand times more easy when they are written. There is also a danger of forgetting your exact goal if it is not written down.

Spending time with your deacons or PCC or leadership team to talk about your church's or organisation's key goals for next year can be very rewarding. You may find not everyone agrees with you! You may also find some ideas far better than your own! So goal sharing is highly recommended, and, to say it again, this is considerably easier if the goals are written down.

Some feel *threatened by such writing of goals*. What if you do not achieve them? If no one knows what you are aiming for no one can criticise you for not reaching it! But you may be criticised anyway for your poor leadership and mistrust of other people. And will you not feel a sense of failure in not reaching a specific target? Maybe, but it depends. If you wanted your church to grow from 220 to 250 members over a year, and a year later you had 249 you probably would not feel too bad. But if you had reached only 221 you would ask what went wrong, and that discussion could almost certainly help you in setting a more realistic goal the following year and enable you to consider your strategy for reaching it.

What kind of goals might be written down? Annually at MARC Europe each staff member is asked to identify up to five goals for the year ahead. One of these can relate to a *consolidation*, that is, building on an achievement of the previous year.

Follow-through and application is thus encouraged. Another goal can be *retrospective*, that is, completing a process begun the previous year. Not every goal runs for exactly twelve months or starts on time and this allows for completion. The other three goals are all *forward* goals, looking into the future and the work that lies ahead. Thus while some goal setting looks backwards, the majority of goals look ahead and are firmly focused on the days to come, not the days past.

Are written goals useful in organisations? Yes, they are. Stated goals from any individual will, if shared, have an impact on other people. They also leave an impact on the organisation itself, reflected not just through individuals' peers, but also their superiors and often their superiors' superiors. It is the individual's personal goals that make the organisation actually 'tick'. Hence it is better for them to be written, shared, known and discussed than to have a series of hidden agendas being worked on.

Reasons for having goals

This is all very well for my church or my organisation, you may be saying, but why should it apply to me? Why should I set goals? And is this book not about priorities? Yes it is, but goal setting precedes priority setting as the earlier diagram made clear. You do need goals, and for the following reasons.

Psychological. Very few of us are self-starters. Most of us need to be helped along the way, and setting goals is one method of doing that. They have a tremendous power to motivate us. But is this not man-focused, and should we not be God-focused? Should the love of Christ not constrain us? Yes, it should and frequently does, but the love of Christ still has to be shed abroad in specific ways. How are you going to show the love of Christ today? this month? this year? This is where goal setting becomes invaluable. Goals help us focus on possibilities and enable us to lift our eyes from immediate, pressing problems. Goals actually help us to achieve our calling and to fulfil our ministry.

Physical. There are only twenty-four hours in a day. We must sleep and eat in that time and have to allocate the rest of our time at work or leisure in the way we feel best. Our priorities are evaluated on the basis of our goals.

Social. We have responsibilities to other people. 'Each one of us should use whatever gift he has received to serve others.'[28] Many of us are part of a larger group, or join with others in a bigger task. Each part of that team helps contribute towards the goal.

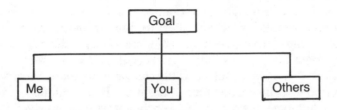

A common goal thus helps create group responsibility. But if a team is to work together in accomplishing an agreed goal, that goal has to be worked out so that each member of the team is involved. As Myron Rush points out, a team is involved in setting goals; a group simply follows the goals of the leader.[29] If we do not know our part, our goal or sub-goal, the whole suffers. We need to work together for the best effect. So often committees are organised around what they do rather than what they are trying to achieve. They lose sight of their goal. After a few years their aims become fuzzy, and an institutional hardening of the arteries sets in: 'What we did last year, plus....' People are asked to join less for their relevant ability and value than for their allegiance to the organisation ('After all, this is *our* church...'). How do you start moving again? Start with yourself and set goals—what do you want to accomplish? Then ask what this church, or this committee is meant to accomplish. Is it being effective? If not, why not? What has to be changed to make it effective? When do I start?[30]

Spiritual. We are called to forget what is behind us and to strive towards what is ahead.[31] Part of our growth towards maturity in the Christian faith is as we 'press ahead'. We need to keep in training ourselves. Biblical imperatives such as 'Be perfect, therefore, as your heavenly Father is perfect'[32] should move us onward. All Christians know they have been called to serve God in some way. Goals help us to focus and to acknowledge that 'we are God's workmanship, created in Christ Jesus to do good works, which God prepared in advance for us to do.'[33]

Goal setting is not, therefore, something which is just an interesting exercise, or possibly useful in some circumstances, but absolutely essential if we are to fulfil all that God wants for us, if we are to become what he intended, if we are to see our vision accomplished. If you want to think through the value of goals, read the extract from William Carey's diary given in Appendix 1, and work out what his goals and vision were.

If you have never set goals before, or even if you have, take time now to fill in the following chart. It deliberately covers areas suitable for both lay and ordained, people involved with churches as well as Christian organisations, spiritual work or secular work. Of the categories listed, choose five and complete a goal statement for each.

	What do I want to happen? (Goal)	When will it have happened?	Hours needed per week
Church fellowship			
Local evangelism through the church			
My family			
Church worship			
Teaching of church members			
My recreation			
Missionary vision in the church			
My personal discipleship			
Service within the local community			
My friends/ neighbours			
My work over the next three months			
My work over the next three years			

Examples of how this diagram might be completed, taken from a MARC Europe seminar on *The Effective Use of Time* are:

	What do I want to happen? (Goal)	When will it have happened?	Hours needed per week
Church fellowship	Extra house group running	By next Easter	½ to organise 3 to carry out
Local evangelism through the church	Organise church members to visit houses on local estate	In one month's time	1 to organise 5 to carry out
My personal discipleship	Reshape my personal prayer diary	By the end of next week	3 hours

We are not just enjoying playing football. We actually want to get that ball in the net, and have the satisfaction of scoring a goal.

Summary

- How we spend our time reflects how we may spend our life: we have to fight for success.
- Our vision is critical for direction—for ourselves, for our church, for our work. What would you like your epitaph to be?
- Our purposes reflect what we want to do, our goals how we want to succeed in doing them.
- Purposes are not measurable; goals are.
- A good goal statement reflects a timed realism, with achievable, specific undertakings.
- Goals look towards the future, are a response to a perceived need, and, in the church, are statements of faith.
- Goals need to be written down.
- We all need goals—for spiritual, social, physical and psychological reasons.

2

I DON'T HAVE ENOUGH TIME

Priorities and how to work them

The Revd Michael Cobley heard the postbox's familiar clanging at 7.15 am. Only eight letters! Three were personal and the other five required his professional action. One was a reply from a minister accepting a pulpit exchange next November: what subject and type of service did he want? Another was from a couple moving into the area: could he please send details of his church and services? A third was from a student with theological queries over a sermon he had heard two weeks ago. A fourth was a cry for help from a family: could he please counsel? The fifth required getting details from the treasurer to send to central office.

As he was reading the post the phone rang. Mr Hewitt, a long-time church member, had had a heart attack: could he please visit him in hospital? He put the phone down, and it immediately rang again: Anthony Roseberry wanted to say his wife had had their baby—a boy, 7 lbs 4 ozs—could he please put the news in the church magazine? This morning was Michael's time for preparing one sermon for next Sunday. He had already promised to visit two elderly people today. Then the phone rang again. It was the minister in the nearby church: could their meeting be moved to tomorrow afternoon?

A knock on the front door at ten o'clock his wife kindly answered: it was someone for the hall key to get ready for the mothers' coffee meeting that morning. Thirty minutes later, however, the next visitor wanted to see the minister: could he please help him as he was feeling so depressed. 'Is God really there?' he said.

This fictitious example reflects something of the pressure many ministers live under. It is important to know how to handle correspondence and interruptions, but handling them well depends on correctly identifying your priorities. What is it you actually want to achieve—in general, in the next year or so, this month, today? This chapter looks at how you may sort out the many claims on your time.

The importance of prioritising

James Woudhysen might be able to write, 'The pinnacle of success and play in the 1980s was to be in control of your time.'[1] But time control for what purpose? In writing about the need for increased grace to meet increased years of our life, Janice Wise said:

> Because God knows the number of our days and their purpose, He wants to direct us so that we can come to old age without regret. He wants us to come to the day of our death knowing that we have done the work God gave us to do, enabling us to say, as Jesus did, 'It is finished'[2].[3]

Our purpose in living must be to accomplish God's purposes for us. But this has to be worked out through resolving our priorities.

Our calling or vocation or vision reflects our values and our deepest desires for our life. How to ascertain these is described in Chapter 4 of *Vision Building*.[4] Our purpose and goals reflect our calling and also, in part, our work context, whether in a church, or a commercial or Christian organisation. Our priorities are determined primarily in our jobs, but not totally so. *Priorities are those goals which, because of their urgency and importance, will receive the greatest prominence in the leadership's thinking and actions.*[5]

One Anglican church minister kept a detailed record of how he spent his time in his church duties over several weeks. If you have never done this you may well find it instructive. The results of his analysis of how he spent his time was as follows:

Time Breakdown of a Minister's Diary

	Total percentage %	Average time in minutes per occasion
Services	21	70
Home visits	20	40
Meetings	16	115
Study/preparation	15	85
Administration	12	240
Chaplain duties	8	125
Deanery duties	5	170
Magazine preparation	3	125
Total	100	105

This particular clergyman worked on average fifty-three hours a week excluding meal breaks. Services included both Sunday and weekday services. Home visits related to pastoral visits, funeral or baptism preparation, home communions, and so on. Many types of meetings were necessary: social committee, youth group, the PCC, and meetings for stewardship, staff, worship, mission, local fraternal, ecumenical gathering and with the bishop. On average these lasted nearly two hours each. A sixth of his time was spent in meetings. The breakdown can be represented in a pie chart:

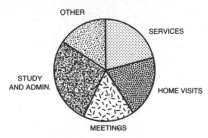

Fig 1: A minister and his time

The value of such information is that it enables the broad parameters of duties to be assessed and evaluated. A key problem identified by Carl George for some ministers was 'What to do with one's time on a daily basis. The trouble with time is that no one holds pastors accountable for it. They can wallow ineffectively day after day, their actions not really adding up to anything in particular, and no one notices.'[6] Noting what you do with your time prevents such problems and also lays the basis for planning each week's work.

Knowing how much time each component takes on average also helps in determining priorities: what you should do today depends on how much free time you have. Carl George went on to say, 'There are two dangers for pastors: spending too much time getting ready for Sunday, and spending too little time.'[7] Balancing between an optimum quality of sermon and service and optimum involvement with people is essentially a priority problem. It is quite possible to spend too much time visiting people as well as too little: some evidence suggests that shorter visits can be more effective than longer ones.[8] Gordon MacDonald, pastor and author, warns of spending too much time on VNPs—Very Nice People who are kind and sympathetic but who enjoy rather than share your passion.[9]

Your top priority

What, then, should one do first? When he leads the MARC Europe seminar 'The Effective Use of Time', Bryn Hughes often points out some of the biblical imperatives including the word 'first':

> *First* be reconciled to your brother, and then come and offer your gift.[10]
> But seek *first* the Kingdom of God and his righteousness.[11]
> *First* remove the plank from your own eye.[12]
> This is the *first* and great commandment.[13]
> But *first* he must suffer many things and be rejected by this generation.[14]
> For if there is *first* a willing mind.[15]

Honour your father and mother, which is the *first* commandment with a promise.[16]

Let them *first* learn to show piety at home and to repay their parents.[17]

In one issue of the *Harvard Business Review*[18] there appeared the story of an educational charity which assigned a young field worker to Peru. He supervised the construction of schools in rural, hard-to-reach areas, and after 2 years had seen 200 new classrooms built at a very low cost. But when the director of the agency came to visit him they found that neither literacy nor school attendance had improved. The young field worker was devastated—was his contribution to Peruvian education a total failure? What was the prime priority?

Personal priorities

What is your prime priority? Here are three that you cannot delegate to anyone else, and for which you alone are responsible.

Your time with God. Whether you rise like Mother Teresa at 4 am each morning for Mass, or spend time in daily devotions some other way, or regularly participate in Communion or other services, your relationship with God is your duty and no one else's. Others may encourage you, guide you, help you, but ultimately your daily discipline of walking with God is yours alone.

Your time with your family. Whether you are single or married, childless or a parent, old or young, part of your basic priority in life is to relate to your relations. In this context this means not just your spouse and children, but your brothers and sisters, parents and grandparents, aunts and uncles, cousins, nephews and nieces. No one else can take your place in your relationship with each of these: you alone are responsible.

Your time working out your vision. Your vision is precisely that—and not anyone else's. The Scriptures do not record anyone having the same vision twice, except perhaps Ezekiel by the River Chebar when he appears to see the throne of God in analogous ways in both chapters 1 and 10. You cannot delegate

working out your vision. Although working at it may not con-
sciously be a daily activity, it certainly ought to reflect your
monthly and annual activities.

Effective time management relates to many things: setting
goals, knowing your vision, handling interruptions, reading
papers quickly, handling crises efficiently, long-term planning,
motivation, evaluation, delegation and procrastination, and priorities—your top priority and your total priorities.

Your total priorities

Priorities relate to you as an *individual*. Your time with other
people, your time with yourself, your time spent planning, your
time with God, your time with your family, your time doing
everything else are all aspects of your life. Time for yourself is
specially important. A friend of mine once said, 'My husband
was always wanting to talk with me. I found it frustrating as I
never had space for myself.' People relax in different ways.
What do you do: play golf or squash; walk; read; knit; collect
stamps; do jigsaws? It does not matter, so long as you find some
time in a busy week when you can really relax and enjoy what
you do.

Priorities also relate to your *work* and *your church*. If you are
a minister you need specially to keep a time for leisure, as your
day off. One study found that only 85 per cent of ministers in
Great Britain took their day off. Are you one of them or are
you one of the 15 per cent that do not?[19] If you are a lay person
your vocation may not be so explicit. As someone once said:

> There is a sense of journey into the unknown and an
> openness to the opportunities that beckon but which nor-
> mally cannot be anticipated. Thus it implies a process of
> ongoing assessment about your talents and gifts, strengths
> and weaknesses, commitments and constraints, and about
> the opportunities or calls on one's time, talents and energy
> which emerge in the normal course of events.

Resolving priorities is necessary in all three areas simultaneously: personal, work and church (or leisure). Each area has its own triangle in this diagram, but the three triangles form a single triangle of priorities:

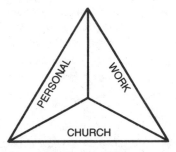

Fig 2: Priorities

Sorting out your personal priorities in isolation can lead to disaster unless you organise all your priorities. One of the greatest difficulties Christian people have in establishing priorities is understanding that we must deal with the whole man or woman. If we believe that all our actions and opportunities are somehow related to the grand purposes of God, then all our life must reflect a consistent view that personal goals—what we should do and what we should be—need to be considered alongside the work goals God has given us.[20]

Priorities need to be established to identify the order in which your goals should be undertaken (you cannot have priorities unless you have goals to prioritise!) and to fit into God's strategy as an effective servant. They reflect your basic value system.

Priorities in context

As you seek to set priorities for your life, four elements must be taken into account, as reflected in the following diagram.

History. Each of us has a unique history. Your history—your knowledge of your gifts, skills, and personality traits—is bound to be a factor in setting your priorities. If you can never get up before 7.30 am you may decide to set your priority as learning to get up at, say, 6.00 am. On the other hand you may be the

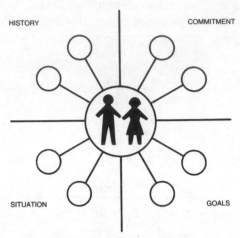

HISTORY

COMMITMENT

SITUATION

GOALS

Fig 3: Priorities in context

kind of person who works much better late at night, so your priority will focus on what you will do at midnight. If you can speak French fluently this may well influence your priorities. If you are afraid of heights, you will probably not put being a window cleaner as your top priority.

Commitment. Your commitments will shape your priorities too. Have you too many commitments? On how many committees do you sit? (One person at a MARC Europe seminar sat on thirty-eight!) Is a sixth of your time spent at meetings, like the vicar whose diary was analysed earlier? Is that level of commitment right for your priorities? In 1985 Owen, a friend of my eldest son, was tragically killed in a cycle accident. At his funeral several letters to his mother were read out, including one from an elderly lady whom Owen had visited on the second Tuesday evening in every month since he was ten. Sometimes he just talked with her, sometimes he played a game, or went for a walk, or took her shopping. 'I feel as though I've lost my own son,' she wrote. Owen had a commitment which he honoured every month for over seven years and which affected his priorities.

Your present *circumstances,* or environment, are bound to

affect your priorities also. You may exclaim, as did one Baptist pastor, 'If only I had a different set of deacons!' but the reality is that you do not (yet!) and therefore have to work within the possibilities set by your current people. Organisations' circumstances and priorities tend to change more slowly and less frequently than individual, personal priorities. One Canadian church was run by eight couples who sat on all the key committees and never thought of asking anyone else to help. Their time was so fully occupied they could not cope with a request for an extra prayer meeting. Eventually that church closed. They had followed a wrong set of priorities.[21]

When the American baseball favourite, Yogi Berra, was asked to speak at a special father-and-son banquet, he gladly signed bats and balls given to him by the youngsters present until he noticed a group of lads who had no gifts. Inquiring, he found they were from the local orphanage, and left the head table to talk with them and sign their programmes. When asked to return to speak he said, 'Go on with the programme. I am busy talking to my friends.'[22] Little things mean a lot.

Goals. What is it you wish to accomplish? What do you wish to be thanking God for in ten years' time? As a member of College Hill Presbyterian Church in Northern Ireland once asked the pastor, Jerry Kirk, 'What would you be attempting for God in College Hill if you had no thought of failure?'[23] Such concerns are relevant for the short term as well as the long term.

Resolving priorities

No one way of resolving priorities works in every situation, or with every person. The needs of others are different from yours perhaps, and your long-term needs will vary from those relating to the shorter term. Some priorities can be established on a single principle, others entail several simultaneously. These two aspects of complexity and time span will be used to identify four types of solution, as reflected in the following diagram:

Complexity

	Simple	Multiple
Shorter term	Basics	ABC
Longer term	80-20	Grid

Basic commitments

This simple criterion is relevant to shorter-term priority evaluation, although its roots are longer term. Christian people have three essential commitments, summarised in the following list:

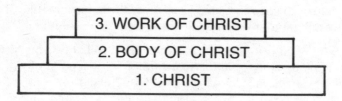

3. WORK OF CHRIST

2. BODY OF CHRIST

1. CHRIST

Christ. Personal encounter with Jesus Christ is fundamental for every active Christian person. He determines our values and our actions. 'You are what you do, not what you believe.' The priority of that commitment needs to be reasserted each day as we determine what we should do and what sort of person we should be.

Body of Christ. This reflects our priority in our relationships to our brothers and sisters in the family of God. We did not choose each other! It will reflect our times with our relations, times meeting others in the church, our times of fellowship, of learning such as in Bible groups, and our service. We reflect our affiliation to the church's people and make time for others built on the same foundation.

Work of Christ. If we are Christian 'professionals' this is usually defined as our paid work—a very limiting concept! If we work in a secular capacity it reflects our involvement with the programmes of our church. Pope John Paul II once said, 'Don't let the work of the Lord come before the Lord of the work.'

These three basic priorities may be summarised as God-People-Work, and this simple order can sometimes guide in priorities. Suppose someone asks if he can see me for a few minutes before I leave, and I have a calculation to complete also prior to going home. If I have time for only one of these two, which do I do? By applying the God-People-Work principle, I would talk to the member of staff; people's needs come before work needs. People matter more than things.

This gives a quick mechanism for sorting priorities in the heat of the moment when many things may be happening. We also have to be sure, however, that our desire to help people does not interfere completely with the task to be done. When the crowd came in acclamation to Jesus, He moved on to other towns to preach the kingdom of heaven there also. Although He frequently allowed people to interrupt His movements, He still kept to the purpose of His coming. So must we.

If you want to see how far you are following these three commitments, take your diary for the last week, analyse each engagement and enter it in the appropriate box in the following diagram.

Commitment to Christ	Commitment to the Body
Commitment to Work	Other Commitments

How balanced are your activities? How much do they reflect your goals, your values, your visions? If they do not, what changes will you now plan for next week's activity?

The 80–20 rule

This concept was first described by a nineteenth-century economist called Pareto. It is essentially simple, even if geared for a longer-term solution: what actions produce the relatively greatest effect?

The 'rule' means that 80 per cent of your effectiveness comes from 20 per cent of your activity, and therefore the remaining 20 per cent of your effectiveness comes from 80 per cent of your activity. The principle applies in many cases. For instance, 80 per cent of a firm's sales go to 20 per cent of their customers, 80 per cent of a church's income comes from 20 per cent of its people, and 80 per cent of cars are made by 20 per cent of the manufacturers. Or 80 per cent of your problems come from 20 per cent of your members, and 80 per cent of your success or creativity comes from the few important decisions you make in the hour or so spent each day being specially productive.

Although it is often called a 'rule', the implication of something so hard and fast is false. The numbers are approximate, and may be 90–10 or 60–40 in some instances. It is the marked imbalance of two things which underlies the 'rule', not the precise definition.

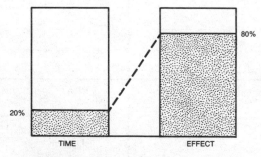

Fig 4: The 80–20 rule

In working out priorities do things which have the greatest effect. You should know your key gifts, the most important skills you have acquired, the best of the experiences you have had; spend your time making use of them. Do not move to a job where these skills have no room to flourish. Stay longer in a job where you have the opportunity to use them. We are called to work as effectively as we are able. Here is a way of translating that calling into a week-by-week calling of our activities. Spend some of your time doing what you do most effectively. Alan Lakein, an author whose books on time management have sold in their millions, crystallises this concept with the question, 'What is the best use of your time right now?'[24]

How can you work effectively? Myron Rush has some practical advice in his book *Burnout*:

> Focus on minimising or eliminating the many activities in your day that take up so much of your time yet produce such a small part of your overall result. If you think you don't have enough time to spend with your family, begin to eliminate the activities in each week that contribute little to your productivity. You can find time for your family and still get all the important things done as well.[25]

Are you good at solving problems? Then be encouraged. One person felt unappreciated until he found this note on his desk: 'Be thankful for the problems—if they were less difficult, someone with less ability would have your job.'[26]

The ABC technique

This simple method for dealing with multiple activities can often be helpful for sorting out a mass of things to be done each day. My long-suffering secretary is asked to handle many items. 'Which should be done first, Peter?' she cries when she is overloaded. We frequently use this technique to resolve that question.

First make a list of things you have to do. You can buy sheets already printed for this purpose, or photocopy the grid below:

Things to do

1 _____

2 _____

3 _____

4 _____

5 _____

6 _____

7 _____

8 _____

9 _____

10 _____

11 _____

12 _____

13 _____

14 _____

15 _____

Some people prefer to write each task on a separate piece of paper, which can then be thrown away when that task is done. The pieces of paper can always be reshuffled the next day to reflect changing priorities. But be careful. An H. Martin cartoon shows a man sitting at a desk covered by notes of things he should be doing. A colleague is talking to him, and the seated man says, 'Let me take a note of that. I can't do anything unless it is written down.' So much to do and all his time was spent writing it down. But in truth, it is no laughing matter—we are fighting for time.

Having made such a list, check first that each is a proper goal (a timed measure of a stated performance) and also ask the following questions of each:

How urgent is it? Must it be done today? Or just soon? Or

maybe sometime? (Can that magazine article not wait till tomorrow? May I not plan that next week?)

How important is it? Very important? (Yes, I must go to the bank today!) What weight does the item have in your values? Are the people asking you to do something particularly important? (Yes, the bishop wants this done this week!)

A sports coach came to a new understanding of her priorities, and in describing her changed attitudes said:

> I learned not to let the urgent get in the way of the important. The urgent is the paper work on my desk, my appointments, my daily routine. Some of my coaching responsibilities. The important is my faith, my family, my friends and my relationships with my players. I'm still learning, but with time I am getting my priorities in the right order.[27]

How often must this be done? Every day? Every week? Just occasionally? (That pastoral visit? Going to the dentist?)

Can someone else do this more effectively than I can? Often when the answer is 'yes' to this question we still do not hand it over because we greatly enjoy doing that particular job, perhaps because it requires a special knack to it, or an unusual skill. But delegating it allows someone else to learn and gives you more time to do other things, including new things yourself. (How to delegate is discussed later.)

Is it part of a larger task I am committed to? Will it contribute to your long-term goals? (If you want to be a missionary in Brazil it is sensible to spend time learning Portuguese. A part-time course will help you qualify as a cost accountant in due season.)

What will happen if it is not done at all? Will anyone notice? ('So you missed choir practice!' How much does that really matter?) But some things not done, or done too late, can lead to disasters, like Chernobyl.

Having asked these questions and deleted or amended items on your list accordingly, what then? Go through the items looking for those which are of greatest importance or highest value and mark them A. Then go through and mark items which are not important and have a low value with a C rating. All those which are then not marked A or C must be B: things you should do, are fairly important and have medium value.

Frequently in such an exercise too many activities get labelled A. Go through these and label them AA, AC or AB. Your prioritics then are to follow—in order—the AA tasks, and when completed the AB, then the AC, and if there is any time left over the B tasks and the C tasks. Tomorrow, repeat the exercise but recategorise the priorities according to any change in circumstances.

An example of how this might work is given in the list below, taken from the earlier exercise for ministers, with the answers as generally given at MARC Europe seminars.

Things to do

Visit three nearby families next week who don't go to church.	A	AA
Preach on the subject of world mission at least twice in the next six months.	B	
Prepare next two sermons with twenty-four hours to spare.	A	AC
Restrict my committee membership to five.	B	
Lead a party to the Holy Land the year after next.	A	AC
Enrol on a rapid reading course by the end of the month.	C	
Spend extra fifteen minutes in prayer every day for six months starting next Monday.	A	AA
Move to a larger church in three years' time.	C	
Phone or write to my brother/sister every two weeks for the next six months.	B	
Read one chapter in a book on management every day for the next month.	A	AB

The priorities are:

> visiting
> praying
> reading
> preparing
> leading
> preaching
> restricting
> phoning.

One rarely has time to do the Cs!

Write down now the things that you have to do tomorrow, large or small (use the blank grid given earlier if you wish) and identify your A priorities, then your Cs and Bs. Repeat with the As if necessary. Now follow the order shown! That is what prioritisation is all about. But do one thing at a time. Lord Chesterfield wrote to his son in 1747, 'There is time enough for everything in the course of the day if you do but one thing at once; but there is not time enough in the year if you will do two things at a time.'

The urgent and the important

Ultimately priorities focus on two areas—time and value. How quickly must something be done? How important is it? On the answers to these two questions lie virtually all the directions to a person's priorities. US General Dwight Eisenhower is reputed to have said, 'I make sure that only the urgent and the important cross my desk.' To help think through such answers a simple grid focusing on these two aspects is given below, with each area broken into two parts.

Box A indicates an activity which is both highly urgent for you and personally very important. It has got to be done quickly and done correctly, as far as you are concerned. What should your reaction be? Very simple: *Do it at once*, or at least schedule it for very immediate action.

Box B indicates that something is personally highly important but does not have to be done immediately. What then do you do? You *plan it!* How this may be done is explained in the

Personal priorities

URGENCY

		LOW	HIGH
I M P O R T A N C E	LOW	D	C
	HIGH	B	A

next chapter, but the need for personal planning arises when you want to be sure something goes as well as it can and you have time on your side. One of the personal priorities mentioned above was 'time to plan'. It is crucial that every church leader puts time aside, perhaps two or three days a month, to plan the way ahead, whether short-term assignments such as the next month's services, or longer-term objectives or goals for church or organisation.

The box labelled C represents a task that has to be done quickly but is not critically important to you personally. Where you have someone available, therefore, the best action is to *delegate it*. For those in an office or management structure in a Christian organisation, delegation may be relatively easy. For many ministers, especially those working with several churches, it is not so simple. But part of the function of a church is to help its members to grow, and people have the opportunity of growth as they are encouraged to take action. You may need to persuade somebody to try something, you may need to teach them how to do it, but eventually delegation saves you effort— and you have taken one further step in the process of building your team. Patience and understanding are two of the disciplines of delegation. *Always* delegate things you cannot do.

Invariably delegate things which are not part of your primary goals, tasks or priorities.[28]

Good team management is reflected by *clear delegation*. Bryn Hughes has helpfully summarised the essential features of good delegation (these are expanded in the chapter on time management):

- Give precise and accurate requirements concerning the task. Many organisational hiccups are caused by poor quality communication in this area. The time span available must be made clear, and even on subjective topics, standards should be defined as precisely as possible.
- Delegation does not mean abdication, but authority must be delegated parallel to responsibility. Make sure that the boundaries are understood, especially on aspects such as confidentiality, equipment, finance, etc.
- Do not do everything for them but give ideas and sources of the relevant information.
- Allow people to make mistakes. This is one of the best ways of learning.
- Make clear when you require interim progress reports and when you are available for further consultation. Reports could be at regular dates or at stages of the task.
- Accept responsibility for all delegated decisions. Especially in public, let your support be openly seen. If a mistake has been made, allow the person to reverse it, but do not countermand it yourself.

Box D reflects an action which, as far as you are concerned, is not important and has no urgency attached to it. What should you do? *Forget it!* Why spend your time in doing something which does not matter and which can be done any time?

If you are a minister and want to have a valuable discussion with your PCC, elders or deacons, or if you are working in a Christian organisation and want to have a similar fruitful discussion with your departmental heads, list all the key activities in which your church/organisation is involved. Then draw the grid given above and allocate each item to one of the boxes. If unanimity is difficult to achieve, take a simple vote. Look at where each activity is assigned—what should you do as a consequence? Are any in box D? Should they be scrapped? Are all in box A? If so, help! A church/organisation should have between three and six key activities, and if you have more than that either they are misclassified or you have a leadership crisis or you need a lot more delegation. All are possible!

The A box can be broken down further, if necessary, and sometimes it is helpful to do that.

<table>
<thead>
<tr><th></th><th colspan="2">HIGH URGENCY</th></tr>
<tr><th></th><th>SHORT-TERM</th><th>LONG-TERM</th></tr>
</thead>
<tbody>
<tr><td>MINOR</td><td>Z</td><td>Y</td></tr>
<tr><td>MAJOR</td><td>Y</td><td>X</td></tr>
</tbody>
</table>

HIGH IMPORTANCE

Looking at the A activities in this way is equivalent to categorising them AA, AB, or AC in the previous system. Again, completing this box forces answers to the questions of time and value, not now in terms of whether the activity is essential or non-essential, but in terms of the degree of cruciality. Box X items are usually easier to distinguish, and it can be argued about which Y box is more important. Box Z in this context is least important, though still valued enough to be there. Critical action tends to focus on the X box; that is, your basic priorities as a church/organisation are driven by activities of high long-term urgency and of major importance. This is precisely what it should be.

Applying priorities

Priorities for the local church

How best can a pastor set priorities for his church? That depends on what the church is there for. What are the main activities of your church? The Chicago urbanologist and pastor, Ray Bakke, in *The Urban Christian*, defines them as six: to provide worship, fellowship, nurture (or training or discipleship), evangelism (at home), mission (in the overseas sense), and service (to the local community). No parachurch organisation ever seeks to do all six, but every church implicitly or explicitly should do them all. You could put all six straight into box A, but that is not very helpful. Rather identify each item's major components. Worship, for example, clearly includes the provision of the Sunday services, but will entail more than that—perhaps the weekly choir practice, or the demonstration in people's everyday lives of their joyous relationship with their heavenly Father through Christ. Ask your leaders: what do we hope to achieve in each of these areas by the time of our next business meeting, or annual general meeting?

There are other ways of describing the key activities of the local church. John Stott, former Rector of All Souls Church, Langham Place, London, described his vision for the church as having five features: it was to be a biblical church, a worshipping church, a caring church, a serving church, and an expectant church.[29] The Revd Paul Beasley-Murray's dream for his church is a worshipping church, a biblical church, a praying church, a Spirit-filled church, a family church, an evangelising church, and a liberated church.[30] At a leadership seminar in 1991, Professor Eddie Gibbs suggested that 'the purpose of a local church is to teach, to care, to win, to go, to listen and to co-ordinate.' The flow chart given earlier shows goals before priorities; these elements cannot be prioritised easily without knowing the goals first.

How far any church adopts these activities will depend partly on what is expected of the leader, and that in turn should be reflected in a job description. That helps to clarify the call, assign priorities, and give relevant boundaries. An example is given in Appendix 3 for an Anglican clergyman, but many other denominations' requirements will be similar.

Priorities for the organisation

Those working in a company or organisation should know why it exists. What is its fundamental purpose? What is its mission?

What is its current vision? They should also be able to relate their particular responsibilities to such a framework. People are vital to success, so some of the basic priorities in an organisation relate to the mechanics of personnel management.

This is normally worked out through a *job description*. Has everyone a document which indicates the prime purpose and key components of their jobs? People need to know their major result areas, not so much what they should do, but what they should achieve. Job satisfaction is critical, so the values associated with the position need to be both identified and stated. The person to whom the employee is responsible needs to be shown also.

Each individual performance needs to be monitored by *an evaluation* or appraisal, usually once a year. Employees need to know how well they are doing, that is, a focus on the past is required. But a focus on the future is also important— employees need to know where they are going (see 'Writing goal statements' in the previous chapter). Are they critically dependent on others for their success? Will extra training be required to help in realising potential? For what achievements might they receive particular recognition?

Implicit within these priorities is a third: *care for the individual*. This is reflected by employees knowing the work they should be doing in detail, and the best ways of doing it. They should know what experience they will be getting and an indication of where they are headed. Such care extends upwards also. The employer should know what is expected of him/her by those working immediately below. Each individual needs to know how he/she is seen personally, professionally and organisationally. What does he/she want to do (to be)? What is he/she planning to do about it? The individual ought also to know his/her boss's concerns, but he/she is not paid to worry about them! His/her priorities relate to identifying the values which he/she needs to develop to ensure his/her future goals are accomplished.

Priorities for the individual

This chapter has suggested key ways of resolving your priorities. The methods given are applicable in churches and organisations also.

Canon Allan Shatford once said, 'When a man says he hasn't time enough—what he really means is that he hasn't inclination enough.'[31]

Dr Paul Yonggi Cho, leader of the world's largest church, in South Korea, says, 'You can teach what you know, but you'll reproduce what you are.'[32] Where are you in terms of your priorities?

Bill Hybels, pastor of the largest and fastest growing church in Chicago, wrote:

> You don't have to be in business to be over-committed. Women with small children know what it means to do ten thousand revolutions per minute, the speed of a racing motor engine. Pastors, elders, church members operate at the same relentless pace as everyone else. Never a dull moment, never a reflective moment either.
>
> Authentic Christianity is not simply humanitarian service to the less fortunate. It is a supernatural walk with a living, dynamic, communicating God. Authentic Christians are persons who stand apart from others, even other Christians, as though listening to a different drummer. Authentic Christians are full of surprises. That's because authentic Christians have strong relationships with the Lord, relationships that are renewed every day.
>
> Embarrassingly few Christians ever reach this level of authenticity; most Christians are just too busy. A key ingredient in authentic Christianity is time. Not left-over time, not throw-away time, but quality time. Time for contemplation, meditation and reflection. Unhurried, uninterrupted time.[33]

Time for major priorities. What are yours? The Roman poet, Horace, said, 'Carpe diem': Seize the day!

Summary

- Analysing your diary can help show you how you spend your time and the need for allocating priorities.
- The priorities which cannot be delegated for Christians are their time with God, their family, and their vision.
- Priorities inevitably reflect an individual's history, commitments, situation and goals.
- A simple prioritisation is God-People-Work.
- The 80–20 rule suggests we should always spend some time in those areas where we are most effective.
- The ABC technique helps decide our A priorities.
- Value and urgency are the key determinants in allocating priorities.
- Priorities must not just be identified—they have to be acted on!

3

I DON'T HAVE TIME TO WORK IT OUT

Plans and how to make them

Fail to plan and you plan to fail says an old adage. This is very true, as in the following case. Jim Holt had to buy stamps for a circular but was short of cash. In a hurry he dashed out, paid his paper bill, popped into the library and then joined the queue at the post office. When he got to the counter he realised he had not been to the bank first. 'I'll be back in a few minutes,' he said. He was, but had to queue again. Had he stopped to think, or plan, for a few seconds, he would have saved himself many minutes and prevented a feeling of intense frustration. Most of us have had similar experiences.

A survey of captains of industry made in 1985 for the British Institute of Management asked for the most important skills for a manager. The four characteristics receiving the highest responses were:

Leadership	95%
Communication	86%
Entrepreneurship	71%
Organising their time	70%

The last—effectively planning—shows how important this feature is for quality managers, be they in industry, commerce, education or the church.

The need for planning

Plans and goals

Christian planners trust in God's sovereign purposes. 'For I know the plans I have for you, says the Lord, plans for welfare and not for evil, to give you a future and a hope.'[1]

Someone said, 'Planning is thinking ahead to solve a particular problem.'

The planning process brings together two key elements in our use of time: deciding what we have to do and putting these tasks into a logical time frame.

Planning presupposes that we have goals we wish to fulfil, and that we have prioritised them.

What are we wanting to do? Whether we simply need to do some shopping, say, or carry out a more detailed programme of events for the next week, or work towards a larger event or project involving major resources and time, we still have to answer the question, 'What has to be done?' This is the purpose, the vision, the goal statement. We are not asking here why we are doing it, but rather stating the results of the actions we intend to take. If we do not know where we are going, we will probably end up somewhere else!

When does it have to be done? This question gives a time frame to our action statement—the crux of a good goal. We must know when the desired actions will have been completed.

But, you may say, this process does not tell you how you are to accomplish your various goals. This chapter describes two planning techniques which help you to find out.

Why plan?

Good planning is critical for high efficiency. It:

Saves time. Planning takes time too, but it is worth it! It is not true that the harder you work the more you get done. Every hour spent in effective planning can save hours in execution and ensure better results—'Work smarter, not harder.'[2] Usually the more time we put into detailed planning the more actual time is saved, as the following diagram illustrates, and the principle is valid whether time is measured in minutes, hours, or days: with less planning it takes more time to do a job; with more planning it takes less time to do the job, and less time spent overall.

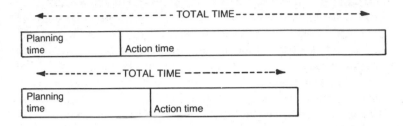

Because planning takes time it should begin as far in advance as possible. If your church year begins in September, do not wait till July to begin organising it, but start in March or April. The time required to plan effectively has discouraged many from attempting it.[3] Do not be discouraged! Keep at it! It yields more time saved!

Aids communication. Had Jim Holt said to his wife what he was going to do before he dashed to the car, she might well have reminded him to go to the bank first. Knowing what has to be done helps us to tell others our objectives.

Guides decision making. Our desire may be to see our church grow in the next year (a legitimate goal) but how we are going to accomplish it is less certain. Planning aids that thinking, and praying, process.

Helps chart the future. When you are travelling to an unfamiliar place you need careful directions as to how to get there. Planning is essentially performing the same role, and helping us improve in the process. 'It is pleasant to see plans develop. That is why fools refuse to give them up even when they are wrong.'[4]

Gives direction. Plans are like an arrow, pointing the way we should go. They are a way of trying to write future history, either short term or long term. We want 'to provide adequate funds so that our children can go to college', 'to begin a new ministry in a ghetto area', or 'to install a new training programme for our organisation'. The point of the planning arrow figuratively touches the goal.[5]

The process of planning tries to take into account God's will. Proverbs 16:9 tells us that 'a man's mind plans his way, but the Lord directs his steps'. 'We need to go down into the plans of God. Go down as deep as you may. Let go with God. You will be led and as a babe is safe in the arms of its mother, so you will be safe with God' said Graeme Irvine, President of World Vision International.[6] As a school governor said to a headmistress caught in a series of problems not of her own making, 'Either you believe in the sovereignty of God, or you don't.' By stating our plans we are identifying what we think He wants us to attempt.

Thinking (and praying) is vital. Antoine Ribond, a successful American industrialist, recommends leaders to bath. He asks, 'What do you do when you take a bath? First you wash yourself. But second you think. You *think*.' He then adds with a wry smile, 'That is the problem with managers today—too many are taking showers; too few are taking baths. No time to think!'[7]

How to begin planning

Planning begins with two key processes: Looking at the NOW: *the way things are*, and stating the THEN: *things as you want them to be* (how your organisation will be in ten years' time, or your church in five years' time for instance—the actual length of time is immaterial). The two ends of the process, the now and the then, are fixed by our present situation and our future objectives. Planning is the mechanism for linking these two elements of the process together.

First analyse your present circumstances—*now*—thoroughly. Here is a series of questions to ask concerning the *resources* that you have. Thinking through the answers to them (a discussion at your team meeting, or with your elders, deacons or councillors can work wonders) often crystallises direction and brings into better focus your future concerns.

Staff. How many staff do you have? How many will you have in, say, five years' time? Categorise them any way you wish: full and part time, ordained or lay, office workers or executives, paid or voluntary (like a non-stipendiary minister), working at home or on the shop floor, travelling or behind a desk, in Britain or overseas, permanent or temporary. How many staff hours are available per week now? How many will be?

Public. Who are your members? Your attenders? Your customers? (Are they young or old? Male or female? Permanent or transitory? Committed or vague? Single or married? Regular or occasional? Active or inactive?) Why do they come to you? What do they really want from you? Where do they come from? What might they be in five years' time? How many people will you have with you then?

Buildings. What buildings do you have? (A church, church hall, office block, shop(s), car(s), key items of specific equipment? Other major fixed resources?) What will you or your organisation have in five years' time? How much frontage do you have? Floor space? How many hours per week is each used now? Will be?

Finance. How much income do you have? How much will you have in five years' time? What is the trend in giving, in donations, in buying, in investing? Does your income keep pace with inflation? Is it decreasing or static? What major items of expenditure do you foresee in the medium term, and are they for maintenance, renewal or expansion?

A similar series of questions can be asked which relate to your *programme*.

Outreach. What are your communication methods now? What will they be in five years' time? What types of printed and/or visual media do you employ? will you be employing? What local programme is there? Do you carry it out alone or in conjunction with others? What types of product do you have available? How might these change? What services do you provide? Are you involved in special missions? Is there a particular anniversary or other key event on the horizon?

Community. What is your community, your market like now? How will it change over five years? How many churches are there? (Is there a new road being built? A prison? A supermarket? Are the people old or young? Rich or poor? Blue or white collar? Is there any incidence of drugs or alcohol addiction? Are there many single parents? Many deaths? Might violence increase? Do people speak your language or another?) What will a visitor note is different five years from now?

Organisation. What kind of leadership structures do you have? Will they change in the next five years? What are your various church groups doing? Will they still be doing the same then? What changes do you see in management levels? (Will your committees still be the same? Your youth work? Your mid-week home groups? Your women's work? Your publications? Will you still have a bookstall?)

Image. How are you seen now by your members? How do outsiders view you? Will either change in the next five years? How does the local press assess your work? How are you seen nationally (if at all)? What relationships do you have with hospitals, schools, youth groups, local and national organisations? What are the key expectations of you? (One church was known as being 'very nice for funerals'.) What reputation would you like to have in five years' time?

Planning for tomorrow is useful not only for groups. Goal setting and planning must become a personal way of life if they are to be truly effective, and subordinate to your vision. Plans must never be isolated from your call. There is a direct relationship between people's effectiveness in their individual life and their effectiveness in their organisational life.

Styles of planning

Different people will plan in different ways. Degree of flexibility is one element: plans can be totally unalterable or easily adapted. Degree of detail is another: some regard it as essential to investigate every item carefully (sometimes very important) while others are content with a broader overview.

These two approaches are summarised in the following diagram:

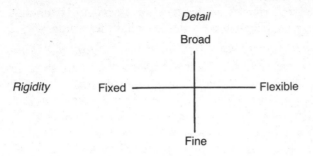

The four areas typify four approaches to planning, as indicated:

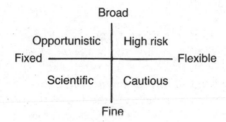

Opportunistic planners. These are involved for the fun of it. They have high energy, good motivation, a willingness to get up and go, often charging like a bull at the gate. Where they are going is less important than the joy and expectation involved in the process. But the ends are fixed, and will not be changed. The enjoyment is often in getting there, but they have only a generally vague notion of what they want to accomplish.

Scientific planners are the reverse: careful, cerebral, and committed to detail. These people do not rush in where angels fear to tread. They think through each item, assess its intrinsic worth. All the 'i's are dotted and 't's crossed in their proposals. All the sums are worked through, and everything is dated.

Cautious planners. These are willing to make a statement or decision only when they are sure it is safe to do so. They are concerned less about direction than deliberation. Unity in decision making weighs more heavily than understanding. Carefulness, rather than correctness, is what they value.

High risk planners. These might well have a different vision every month. The long term is less important to them than the short term. They plan for today, not tomorrow, and therefore do not really plan at all. They judge by the immediate, and not by the implications. Their achievements can be real, but are often temporary. They personally are crucial to the accomplishment; if they should go, the undertaking will probably cease.

Are you one of these four types? The above statements are caricatures, of course, but it is clear that none of the above is ideal. Where would you place the unknown author of these eighteenth-century lines?

> For the want of a nail the shoe was lost,
> For the want of a shoe the horse was lost,
> For the want of a horse the rider was lost,
> For the want of a rider the message was lost,
> For the want of a message the battle was lost,
> For the want of a battle the war was lost.

The author of *Seconds Away!*, David Cormack, likens the above to four types of vessel, respectively, the Viking longboat (opportunistic), the *SS Titanic* (scientific), the Polaris submarine (cautious) and the coracle (high risk). He suggests a fifth approach, as typified by Columbus's *Ave Maria* (organic).[8]

Organic planners. These know where they are going, and are determined to get there. They recognise that problems along the way may cause difficult decisions and temporary changes in direction, but their long-term purpose is secure. They are able to argue this logically and in so doing bind the members of their team with them. The vision is theirs, but the gains are shared. They will take calculated risks where necessary but not needlessly. Firm action may be required but they are flexible in subsidiary matters. Detail is important to them but it does not dominate them. They are leaders more than managers: what is to be done takes priority over how it is to be done. They call, and many will follow.

Human planning and divine sovereignty

Christian people pray over their work believing in the leading of the Holy Spirit. That belief is not obviated by careful planning which is simply a tool to express what the Spirit is helping us to understand and to aid co-ordination of all those involved along the way.

Christians also trust in the sovereignty of God. Man proposes, God disposes. Jesus often called His disciples to come apart and pray. Prayer and planning are alike acts of faith. Planning is a corporate act of faith in the God of the universe. We consider, evaluate and decide what we believe God's will for us is. Planning, like prayer, is hard work. Both need direction by the Holy Spirit. The one is no substitute for the other, and involvement in a complex planning sequence for a Christian without dependence on the guidance of the Spirit is not the way to ascertain God's will for us.

God's plans for projects and bricks and mortar are easily captured in schedules. His plans for people are more difficult to know and follow. Yet His will encompasses both and we need to make ourselves open to Him for both. In that way, planning is held in its correct perspective. How does this work out in practice? Ed Dayton suggests three ways:

- Praying over my things-to-do list each morning
- Expecting that in times of prayer I will receive new ideas or recognise previously unnoticed problems
- Periodically praying with family or colleagues about our goals.[9]

We now need to look at how to put all this into practice. We have to link our dreams, ideas and visions for the future with our history, experience and understanding.

Planning techniques: the portcullis grid

The rigid castle portcullis clearly provides security for those inside. Likewise this particular method of planning emphasises clarity and rigidity. It is a simple, practical and adaptable way of solving many problems. It can be applied as readily in secular organisations as spiritual ones, is universal in its approach and aids understanding of the process.

This particular portcullis has six vertical bars with five spaces in between; it is these spaces which are the key. They can be allocated as follows:

The present. This represents the current situation.

Helps. What are the forces, opinions, actions that will help you reach your goal? What support do you discern? What aid are you likely to get? What is moving you towards your goal?

Hindrances. These are the elements which may prevent you from reaching your goal. What constraints do you envisage? What problems are likely to occur? What forces will be acting against you? What might cause you not to get there?

Plans. These are the steps necessary for you to move forward to your goal. Sometimes it is helpful to think backwards and ask 'What would have to happen before I reached this goal?'

The goal. Where do you want to be, or what do you want to have done in, say, five years' time? What is your objective? Your goal? If it is easier, break it down into sub-goals, on the principle of 'divide and conquer'.

These five steps are not quite the end of the matter but they are the essence of planning. These five areas are best presented in the form of a chart as follows. (You may wish to copy this outline or enlarge to A4 on a photocopier.)

The Present	Helps	Hindrances	Plans	The Goal

The last column (the goal) should be completed first, and then the first column, followed by the second, third and fourth columns.

How it works in practice

An actual example, taken from one of MARC Europe's seminars, is given below. A young Pentecostal pastor wanted to build a new church in three years' time. Currently they worshipped in an overcrowded small building. These two statements are enough to start the process!

The Present	Helps	Hindrances	Plans	The Goal
Overcrowded small building				Build new church in 3 years' time

What did he have to help him? As he spoke, the words were written up on an overhead projector slide—a good technique to use with your leadership team when thinking through plans like this. His answers are shown below, divided into groups to identify key factors:

The Present	Helps	Hindrances	Plans	The Goal
Overcrowded small building	*People* Anxious to change Young congregation with practical skills *Finance* Land available £20,000 in building fund *Other aids* Good local builders Denomination can give skilled advice			Build new church in 3 years' time

He was fortunate to have a pragmatic congregation willing to help with much of the work required to get a building ready—he had plasterers, electricians, and so on, but no architect. He also found that one of his main assets, his people, were also one of his key liabilities. That is not unusual, but it is important to identify why they might be liabilities. They were fixed in their attitude about small details such as the service times, which inhibited alternatives such as having two morning services to alleviate the space problem. Finance was also a potential difficulty, for the £20,000 he did have is quite insufficient to build a new church. So all these problems were listed as hindrances, as shown below.

The Present	Helps	Hindrances	Plans	The Goal
Overcrowded small building	*People* Anxious to change Young congregation with practical skills *Finance* Land available £20,000 in building fund *Other aids* Good local builders Denomination can give skilled advice	*People* No vision Strongly traditional Sunday worship at fixed time Do not perceive need or opportunity *Finance* Building fund not large enough Denomination cannot fund *Other problems* No architect in the church		Build new church in 3 years' time

At this stage you have a grid containing all the crucial elements of a problem. It can therefore be used with others for ideas for solving it. Problem solving implies 'a process by which the learner combines previously learned elements of knowledge, rules, techniques, skills and concepts to provide a solution to a novel situation'.[10] The grid is an ideal way of presenting the issues and was used in this way at a subsequent seminar. 'What would you do if this was your problem?' I asked an all-denominational group of ministers. They made the following suggestions for the 'plans' column:

- Go to the Christian Resources Exhibition to find details about a suitable architect.
- Ask the church to pray about the matter.
- Present the project imaginatively to the church members.
- Establish a fund raising committee.
- Preach a series of sermons on Nehemiah.

Several of these ideas may not have occurred to the Pentecostal minister; this method encourages constructive thinking to facilitate the problem or originate other solutions. The actual solution was interesting: the minister suddenly remembered that the local pub had recently built an extension with a very pleasant layout and finish. So the fourth column was completed with a view to action on this score and with an eye to convincing the congregation of what was to happen.

The Present	Helps	Hindrances	Plans	The Goal
Overcrowded small building	*People* Anxious to change Young congregation with practical skills *Finance* Land available £20,000 in building fund *Other aids* Good local builders Denomination can give skilled advice	*People* No vision Strong traditional Sunday worship at fixed time Do not perceive need or opportunity *Finance* Building fund not large enough Denomination cannot fund *Other problems* No architect in the church	*Aim to get congregational agreement within 12 months* 1) Clarify purposes 2) Formulate building plan 3) Build model of new church 4) Educate congregation *Contact local brewery* Would architect for their recent extension help us?	Build new church in 3 years' time

To show how versatile this method is, and its range from small to large projects, from personal to organisational problems, from short-term to long-term requirements, several completed examples are given, all taken from situations presented at MARC Europe 'The Effective Use of Time' seminars. The first example is of a church in North Wales, and the reference to 'no language problem' reflects the fact that there were many English-speakers in this particular village. How could the vicar (it was an Anglican church) increase the number of families?

The Present	Helps	Hindrances	Plans	The Goal
2 young families only in church congregation (= 4 adults aged 25-40)	*Building* Central location Good heating Big enough to take a crowd *People* Caring leaders Concerned minister Lively worship Existing members involved in church ministry *Outreach* Church magazine distributed widely No other church in village—no competition No language problem Good church school links	*Leaders* Older people in control of PCC No vision for outreach *Worship* No modern music No background noise (parents feel awkward if baby cries) *Outreach* No effective communication to non-church community	Ask the 4 adults in young families to join PCC and act as bridge-builders to older people over next 2 years Then think through programme to reach out to families	20 young families to be church members in 5 years' time

The next example is of a well-known organisation wanting a more streamlined accounting mechanism.

The Present	Helps	Hindrances	Plans	The Goal
Incomplete and infrequent accounts	Recent computerisation of accounts Support of senior staff Extra staff agreed Sound working routines already agreed Part of society's long-term plans	Frequent computer breakdown Accountant has too many interruptions Inertia Some key staff not yet appointed Working routines not followed	1) Convince organisation of the benefits by: —integrating procedures with annual accounts —delegating more of existing work 2) Check routines are —understood —accepted —effective 3) Set aside time each week to plan 4) Break overall task down into sub-goals 5) Get advice on suitable software	Produce monthly departmental and divisional accounts within 2 years to help better decision making

The third example relates to the development of a new branch of the established bereavement organisation, Cruse, in a certain town.

The Present	Helps	Hindrances	Plans	The Goal
No branch	*The organisation* Expanding national organisation Cruse is a caring fellowship with an Open Door Bookshop and bereavement card ministry *Need* Many funerals necessary Many elderly people *Church link* Recently bereaved often susceptible to the gospel Trained bereavement counsellors could be in church	*Community* Growing interest in the occult 'You've got to work it out yourself' attitude No premises available People don't realise church can help at such times *Church people* Lack of vision Yet another bandwagon of the pastor! Insecurity in dealing with those recently bereaved *Time* Needs training programme People want to be involved in more productive evangelistic work Extended church membership already committed	1) Write to Cruse 2) Assess resources 3) Encourage counsellors to come forward 4) Display books on subject 5) Start training programme 6) Visit local doctor, nurses, etc 7) Emphasise quality of intended ministry 8) Share vision with church 9) Pray for God's will 10) Liaise with National Health Service	Establish local branch by end of year in 8 months' time

The next example shows a short-term problem for a church deacon.

The Present	Helps	Hindrances	Plans	The Goal
Haphazard praying for friends and family	Daily newspapers give information List of church members available Own staff known personally Meet people every week during travel as part of employment	Too much information being received Good ideas and details not prioritised	Categorise people to be prayed for—family, friends, staff, casuals, etc Work out a diary system based on these categories Prioritise categories Put names in alphabetical order to prevent duplication Add new information only on those days in which those persons/categories were being prayed for	To create a daily prayer list of people by end of next week

The fifth example comes from some frustrated lay people—this time the problem was how to change the vicar, not the vicar wanting to change the people!

The Present	Helps	Hindrances	Plans	The Goal
Lay person reads one lesson and clergyman the other Lay people take collection and sing in choir but do nothing else	At least 50% of congregation could do something Strong desire to participate Some lay people already involved (in reading)	Older members think 'worship' is vicar's job Vicar is very good at worship Vicar likes leading worship Standards are very high Current participators like their status Pressure of outside commitments	1) Win over PCC 2) Explain value of lay involvement 3) Start general education process 4) Enlarge existing pool of readers 5) Encourage wider involvement at other meetings 6) Identify precisely what vicar likes doing 7) Approach 'core' group and explain 8) Think about the future and continuity 9) Encourage people to ask if they can help	To have 25 congregation members able to participate in worship by reading the lessons, saying prayers, etc, by end of year—8 months' time

The final example comes from Finland, and relates to a widening fellowship in home meetings.

The Present	Helps	Hindrances	Plans	The Goal
Occasional fellowship in homes	Expectations of leader Hosts available and willing Idea of small groups well received Church contacts known Area of influence is discrete Homes often open Local media available Good local worker	Not enough time for fellowship People passive Means more work cleaning home, etc Some pastors not keen because it means church building is used less Some are shy to ask strangers in Some town flats too small Seen as something done in the country, not the town	1) Get information on how other groups are organised 2) Meet to pray 3) Form framework for meeting 4) Give hosts and leaders training 5) Systematically look for suitable homes 6) Co-ordinate with all churches in the town 7) Publicise through local media 8) Send out printed invitations	To establish 80 home fellowships meeting monthly for 4 months, 2 in each parish, within 12 months

Further examples can be found in *The Best Way to Plan Your Day*.[11]

The next steps

Is a suitable list in the 'plans' column the end of the planning process? Not quite, as indicated earlier. Obtaining these ideas and steps is critical, but three further elements are also essential for careful planning:

- Evaluate the time to be taken, the money to be spent, and the effort to be made at each step.
- Give a date for the completion of each step.
- Review progress, and if the above details make the plan unworkable, replan or change the goals! There is no point in attempting the impossible, and this process helps in ascertaining just how realistic your goals are!

This procedure is in fact continuous, not finite as the grids may suggest. In reality aims are not always fulfilled exactly, and we need to reflect this in our subsequent planning. So the sequence of these operations is more adequately illustrated as:

Fig 5: Work is circular

The advantages and disadvantages of the portcullis grid planning technique can be summarised as:

ADVANTAGES	DISADVANTAGES
Methodical and logical	Interrelations of times for each
Identifies all key steps	step not obvious
Facilitates completion of each	Sometimes not succinct
stage	Separate sheet required for
Easy to use with teams	each goal
Helpful to communicate for	
problem solving	
Compact for simple presenta-	
tion	
Allows others to help in prob-	
lem solving	

Planning techniques: the PERT diagram

Although the portcullis grid system involves logical thinking, clarity in conception, and encourages imaginative ideas, it does not help work out the detail of an involved plan. The PERT (Programme Evaluation Review Technique) diagram gives that detail. It can show relationships in very complex programmes, but can be readily adapted to simpler tasks. How far the exact mechanism is followed is less important than realising its key advantages. It:

- imposes a logical order of events and identifies potential hold-ups in advance
- makes the time for completing each aspect overt and available to all
- enables a critical path to be identified, so that if progress along those steps is hindered the eventual outcome will also be delayed.

In many cases working out detail plans does not require the full sophistication of a PERT technique, but the basic concepts can help in the planning even of simple projects.

Long-range planning

PERT is especially used for long-range planning. Long range in a church or Christian organisation context is probably five to ten years. The decadal population census is suitable for central government's long-range planning of its transport, health and education services, and for major industrial multinational companies long-range planning is probably nearer thirty years.

Any long-range plan needs regular updating, however. A good plan is a working document which needs frequent formal appraisal and review. The timing of those reviews should be built in at the outset. Recently, when MARC Europe was rethinking its ministry, its plans were on the agenda for every board meeting (every three months) over a period of twelve to fifteen months. It was automatically a main item on the agenda, and not just a 'matters arising'.

Long-range planning is not forecasting, describing what is likely to happen. It is not concerned with future decisions, but the future of current decisions. Long-range planning does not eliminate risk. We can always be wrong!

Long-range planning, however, does enable us to:

- *Take notice of our existing commitments.* We cannot ignore our history. Our past decisions to some extent regulate present behaviour.
- *Examine the value of our history.* How far are we bound by our past endeavours? How relevant are they for our present ministry?
- *Increase our awareness of our decision-making process.* Who are making what decisions? How are they being recorded? Implemented? Communicated? We must not feel bound necessarily by an out-of-date decision. Every decision is time bound, as in the case of a large building society which promised a substantial donation to a particular organisation, but unintentionally delayed payment over a two-year period. During this time the Society's donating policies changed radically. It was acknowledged that the donation had never been made, but it was cancelled. The decision to give in this case had become out-of-date.

Spell out your vision or your goal statements if you are planning a project over a five- or ten-year period. Most likely there will be several statements or sub-statements. The comments below assume you know your vision. If you do not, the book *Vision Building* may help.[12]

Identify your assumptions critical for the success of your planning and note them down. You may be making assumptions about the intervening period: for instance, that petrol prices will remain fairly constant, or no deathwatch beetle will be discovered, or that you will have adequate funds, or that your key people will not leave.

More than one way of accomplishing your purpose is quite possible. Note these too. They may be helpful in crises and can also show up the impact of variations in policy. Different approaches, alternative courses of action are always useful, if only for reinforcing the agreed line. Sometimes your plans will be wrong. Have the courage to recognise and admit this, and to change direction if necessary.

People and organisation, and their relationship are two of the most important things in long-range planning, not, please note, money. The leader therefore has to have people strong enough to make the plans happen, and to subjugate his/her own personal desires, preferences and ambitions for the good of the whole. On the organisational side, adequate time must be allowed for the detailed planning, with control and review dates built in at regular intervals for analysis, evaluation and replanning if necessary. An Indian proverb says, 'If you are planning for one year, plant rice. If you are planning for ten years, plant trees. If you are planning for 100 years plant people.'

The PERT diagram helps identify your actions more precisely and thus enables the above comments to be more readily worked out, but the key to successful planning is people, not paper. Both, however, are necessary. Jesus said, 'Which one of you, when he wants to build a tower does not first sit down and calculate the cost, to see if he has enough to complete it?'[13] That, if you like, is the paper part. Ed Dayton suggests an interesting theorem relevant to the people part: 'The ability of the Holy Spirit to operate within a local church or organisation is directly proportional to the amount of planning done.'[14]

PERT principles

The key features are as follows:

- Identify
  —all the main actions required for the project to be undertaken
  —all the elements necessary to enable these main actions to be completed.
- For each major and minor activity identify the
  —final date by which it must be completed
  —person responsible for the action
  —probable length of time it will take
  —best case and worst case lengths of time each is likely to take.
- Plot the main activities sequentially in boxes underneath

each other and the minor activities horizontally in boxes in each line.

- Join boxes with lines showing orders of priority taking into account dates for completion.
- The critical path is that chain of events which has the longest probable time of completion.

How it works in practice

As an example,[15] assume that the only activities needed to build a house are as given in the table below, and the most likely times for completing them are as shown, with optimistic and pessimistic lengths, as given. The final column shows the numbers allocated in the diagram to the start and end of each process.

Activity	Time (days)			Event
	Most likely	Optimistic	Pessimistic	
A – Obtain bricks	5	4	7	(0,2)
B – Obtain roof tiles	12	10	15	(0,4)
C – Prepare founda- tions	7	6	8	(0,1)
D – Erect shell	10	9	12	(2,3)
E – Construct roof	4	4	5	(4,6)
F – Lay drains	7	6	8	(1,5)
G – Wire	10	8	13	(3,6)
H – Plaster	6	6	7	(6,7)
I – Plumb	12	10	15	(5,6)
J – Floor	5	4	6	(6,9)
K – Landscape	2	2	3	(8,9)
L – Paint and clean	6	5	7	(9,10)
M – Install doors and fittings	2	2	2	(7,9)
N – Lay pathways	2	2	2	(5,8)

Although many of these jobs can be done simultaneously (such as wiring and plumbing), a logical order is critical: the roof cannot be put on until the shell is erected, nor the plasterers begin work until the wiring is completed, and so on.

A simple way of expressing the various sequences is illustrated below. In the second diagram the activities are replaced by the most likely time they will take.

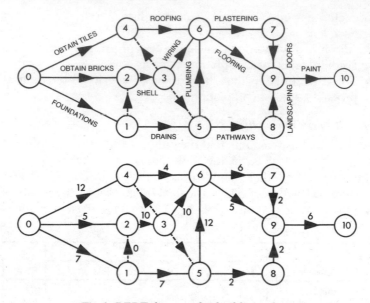

Fig 6: PERT diagram for building a house

This diagram shows that, for instance, the completed shell (circle 3) cannot be built until the bricks have been obtained (circle 2). Once the shell is completed, however, both the roofing (assuming the tiles have been obtained, circle 4) and the wiring can begin, both completed at circle 6. The dotted line represents a 'dummy' activity to ensure correct sequencing; these have 'zero' time between them, that is, they take place simultaneously.

The critical path is given by the sequence 0–3, 5–7, 9–10 with a total completion time of forty-three days. The critical activities are C, D, I, H, M, L, and only a reduction in the time on these can lead to any overall reduction. Likewise a delay in any of these adds to the final completion time.

Other examples

Another example, this time without the detailed explanation of what the circles mean, is of a research survey. The critical path shown in the diagram below (by heavier arrows) relates to the design and testing of the questionnaire.

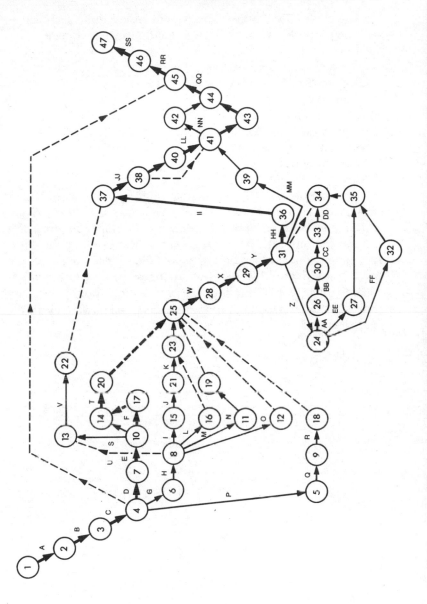

Fig 7: PERT diagram for a research survey

The circles used in the above examples are quite satisfactory for the purpose, but many PERT diagrams use rectangles.

A typical PERT box looks like this: In area A is written the action to be completed and in area B the date by which it must be done and the person responsible for it.

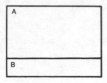

An example of a PERT diagram relating to a Christian task from Ed Dayton's book *Planning Strategies for World Evangelisation*[16] is given opposite (with box B empty except for a reference number). The dotted lines indicate that one event is dependent on another but that no time elapses between the two. It is structured so that box 1 defines the task to be undertaken, boxes 2 to 7 preliminary preparation, box 8 decision, boxes 9 to 19 specific preparation, and boxes 20 and 21 the outcome.

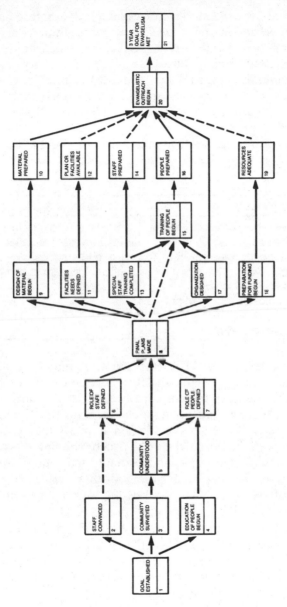

Fig 8: PERT diagram for evangelism

This diagram illustrates, for example, that before final plans for evangelisation can be made the local community needs to be surveyed (box 3) and what they really want needs to be appreciated (box 4). Training (boxes 13 and 15) is necessary before staff and people are ready (boxes 14 and 16). Times for completion are not shown in this diagram. A more detailed explanation of the PERT diagram is given in Ed Dayton's *God's Purpose/ Man's Plans*.[17]

The advantages and disadvantages of the PERT diagram planning technique can be summarised as follows:

ADVANTAGES	DISADVANTAGES
Enables whole project overview to be seen at once Time dependencies easy to see Methodical and logical Communicates totality of project work Highlights critical path	Sometimes too succinct Requires many detailed times and tolerances Difficult for team to complete

Few today use the PERT method mechanically, but its principles are widely available through electronic software for computers. If you need to plan a major project it is much better to get an expert skilled in this field to handle it for you. The principles, however, are explained here so that you can be familiar with the essential issues in such planning.

Planning is important, and planning techniques are useful. More sophisticated planning methods than are described above are available. It is, however, possible to go overboard on the process of planning and forget its purpose. The basic reason for planning is to bring together the work of different people in a harmonised framework. How that is achieved matters far less than that it is achieved. We need to ensure that we do not overplan and squeeze out people's creativity and sense of participation.[18]

Introducing planning

The two methods of planning outlined above give an indication of what has to be accomplished. But until someone actually starts, the process never begins. As a Chinese proverb states, 'He who deliberates fully before taking a step will spend his entire life on one leg.'[19] Another is, 'He who considers everything decides nothing.'

How, then, do we start if we are part of a team, a member or leader of a church, an officer in a organisation? Some people say planning as such is not important but the process of it is. There is an element of truth in this, but I believe both are important. The planning gives you your direction, the process your capability of getting there.

Teamwork

A purpose statement, mission objective or set of goals is essential for your church, your organisation, your business. Planning involves teamwork—more than one person will be involved in the success or failure of the project. Teamwork is a whole subject by itself, but all effective teamwork involves communication—you have to share together to work together effectively. Communication involves knowing where you are going, and a purpose statement helps that process. This is the first key in successful planning.

What actions are needed to accomplish that purpose is the second thing you have to decide. The methods already outlined can help here if your people are sufficiently committed already to work in such a structured manner. What if they are not? Then help them to think towards the future. Suggest, for example, that the annual report or the annual general meeting allocates most of its space or time to what the group expects to happen next year rather than what happened last year. Look forward not backwards.

Many organisations and churches have an annual budget. Ask the people or person responsible for spending to explain the purpose of their expenditure, and then the following year invite them to report on how it went. Or, more imaginatively, make your annual budget a time for suggesting an approximate budget for three or five years' time. This breaks away from the constricting 'here-and-now', the immediate, and moves towards thinking into the possibilities and potentialities of the days ahead.[20]

Build on the existing relationships and the new ones that joint action will create:

- Groups may need training to accomplish their task. Define that training, decide who will do it, and when by, how much it will cost, and where it will be held. Announce these details in relation to what will be accomplished as a result.
- People may need time to think the process through. Organise a weekend away for your group so that people can get to know each other outside the work or functional situation. One vicar always invites his PCC members to mince pies and coffee after the service the Sunday evening before the carol service. Such social occasions aid the rapport of the group. They help everyone get to know each other better and the strengths and weaknesses each one brings to a discussion. Remember, our commitment is to the body before it is to the task.
- Motivation must be discovered. 'My goals are good goals, your goals are bad goals.' What motivates each individual? People are motivated by their perceived needs—what they want to see done. How do you discover those? Try answering for each person in your group questions such as 'What makes them tick?' or 'When does Miss A work with enthusiasm?' or 'What does Mr B do well, do poorly?' Ask yourself what motivates you. What is your vision? Build the plans around these motivations as far as you can.
- Spot your thoroughbreds. Actress Patricia Neal recalled a motto her father had above his desk: 'When you call upon a thoroughbred, he gives you all the speed, strength of heart and sinew in him. When you call upon a jackass, he kicks.'[21] Who are the people who give you all they have? The most reliable and trustworthy? The ones who, by God's grace, will surely get there?

Don't be daunted

Isaiah's majestic words 'Make straight in the desert a highway for our God' are amplified in the following verse with the means: 'Every valley shall be lifted up, and every mountain and hill be made low; the uneven ground shall become level, and the rough places a plain.'[22] However large the obstacle, think of ways of overcoming it.

All planning is a risk. You cannot be sure of getting there, but you can be absolutely sure you will not get there if you do not keep going. If you do not know how far you can go, go as far as you can, and you will then see better the way ahead. Planning statements are statements of faith, and Christians are called on to have great faith. It takes little faith to take a little risk.[23] Exactly so! How great is your faith? What risk will you take? Will you go all the way so that your plans may be fulfilled? Lee Iacocca, the American motor car magnate, says, 'If you take no risks, you do nothing.'[24]

This process of not being daunted can be helped by planning. The following diagram is explained in more detail elsewhere,[25] but is repeated here to show how planning helps keep direction.

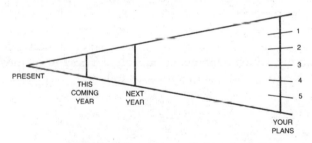

Fig 9: Looking to your future plans

Each of your future plans, say the five main thrusts to your project, has some link with the present, if only an indication that more detailed work will be needed on it in time. Represent these links with lines joining your future plans to the present. The diagram then looks like this:

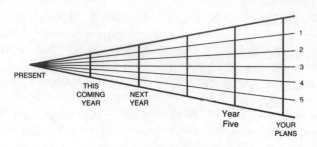

Fig 10: Planning with thrusts

Not every thrust lasts for the whole time period. That does not matter. Keep the line in, but it represents zero activity when that particular aspect is completed.

In the process of fulfilling your plans, someone may have an idea. ('Wouldn't it be a good idea, pastor, to visit everyone in the parish with mince pies to encourage them to come to the carol service?') The pastor may agree, and the idea is added to the scheme of things. Appropriate time, money and people are allocated. Someone else, realising that money is a problem, suggests that the minister does a sponsored parachute jump. The minister considers the idea and wonders if the image of parachuting clergy will actually enhance the work. As it does not, he declines, irrespective of his personal preferences for parachutes, which need never be stated! These ideas might be called X and Y and would appear as follows:

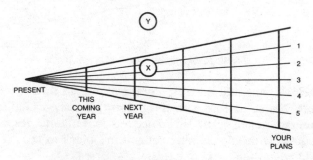

Fig 11: Planning and developing ideas

The first idea is contained within the plans. You accommodate it and use it and in so doing are not diverted from your task. The second is outside your designs and is rejected as a consequence. Detailed planning in this way aids your decision.

The following simple example reflects the value of having a plan to which you are working, with its broad steps clearly defined. Changes necessary within that plan can then be much more easily understood and accommodated.

Southeast Asian Outreach is a small missionary and relief organisation which agreed with the Cambodian government on a fish farming project. This involved research and building a dam to control the pool in which the fish would be cultivated. The plan was clear and approved, but not all the funding was available, and one person on the governing committee felt strongly against going ahead with building the dam. As another member prayed over the situation he realised the order in the plan was wrong. Rather than build the dam and then the house for the fish research, the house should be started first; enough funds were available for building that. Such a diagram as that above meant that the overall plans were not changed—no diversion—but the order of events was amended.

Imagination

Often helping people to see in their mind's eye the process or the dream helps plans to work. Displaying visually what you are planning frequently helps. This might be done with pictures (an item worked through in more detail elsewhere[26]), but can sometimes be just as excitingly conveyed by a list or a flip chart—pin the sheet on your notice board, or type it up and circulate it just as a list for comment. This list of ideas as to what the future church might achieve came from one leadership conference:[27]

> Having a restored voice in the nation's affairs
> Having a vision to reach the 80 to 90 per cent of people outside the church
> Having its own house in order
> Having a strong involvement in overseas mission
> Having an effective voice in people's lives
> Having an image of relevance to ordinary people

Being cohesive
Having national unity in fellowship
Being bigger
Being more biblical
Recognising congregational gifts
Recognising women's gifts
Being practically and effectively evangelistic
Being uncompromised
Holding young people
Being 'homogenised'
Having effective leaders
Taking relevant initiatives, eg, with the unemployed/marital breakdown/race/urban renewal
Being non-aligned by class or ethnic group
Re-establishing the liturgy
Reforming the House of Bishops
Overcoming Victorian architectural constraints
Communicating and using the media effectively
Demonstrating radical holiness
Continuing experiments with new forms of worship
Planning and managing in a godly way
Ending need for Christian societies (because of greater synthesis)
Having independent voice, that is, Church of England disestablished
Having more realistic financial support
Having more committed and more disciplined membership
Encouraging variety and tolerance
Having greater understanding of the alternative morality
Having closer world-wide fellowship
Having more involvement with overseas churches.

The Overseas Missionary Fellowship has an internal flow chart describing the processing of candidates. This is shown opposite, but to help everyone externally understand the process they illustrate it as shown on the following page.

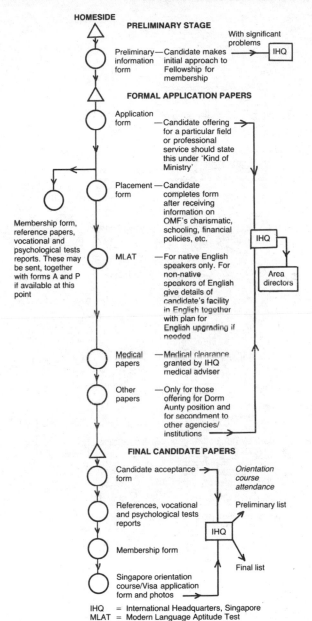

Fig 12: How the Overseas Missionary Fellowship processes applicants

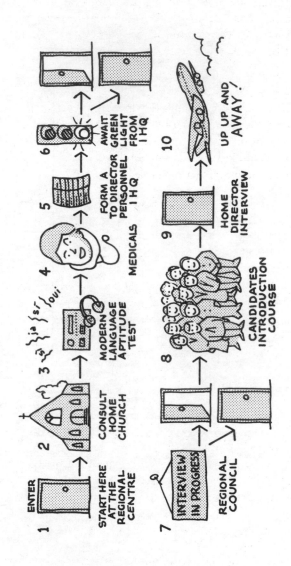

Fig 12: How the Overseas Missionary Fellowship processes applicants

The major processes

If, therefore, you are introducing planning to your church, your organisation, your department, what are the key steps to be taken? David Cormack, Associate Director of Training with MARC Europe, lists the following seven points:[28]

- Talk about it.
- Involve others.
- Look for ways of building on existing concerns.
- Gradually push the horizons out.
- Gather around you a group of enthusiasts on whom you can depend to think forwards sensibly.
- Focus on forecasts, not reports.
- Establish a process of review.

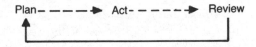

To these I would add the crucial commitment to not being diverted from your intent. Someone once said, 'Do not be afraid of going slowly; be only afraid of standing still.'

How to get started? Baptist pastor, Stephen Gaukroger, listed useful questions about each group in your church or organisation in *Leadership Today*:[29]

1 What was its original purpose?
2 What is its aim now?
3 Is it accomplishing its aim?
4 If not, why not?
5 Could anything else accomplish these aims more effectively?
6 What are your dreams for this group at its best?

Machiavelli wrote in *The Prince* in 1513:

There is nothing more difficult to carry out, nor more doubtful of success, nor more dangerous to handle, than to initiate a new order of things. For the reformer has enemies in all who profit by the old order, and only lukewarm defenders in all who profit by the new order. These lukewarmers arise partly from fear of their adversaries, who have law in their favour; and partly from the incredibility of mankind, who do not truly believe in anything new until they have actual experience of it.[30]

We need to recall Paul's affirmation to the Christians in Thessalonica: 'Faithful is he who calls you, who also will do it.'[31]

Summary

- Planning presupposes we know where we are going.
- Planning saves time.
- It does not obviate God's will.
- Planning bridges the gap between the way things are now and things as we want them to be in several years' time.
- Different types of people use different styles for planning.
- The portcullis grid identifies the favourable and unfavourable items behind reaching your goal.
- The PERT diagram shows you the critical part of key events which must be completed on time.
- All types of planning require regular review.
- Successful planning involves teamwork, objectives, and good communications.
- It is crucial to spot key people.
- Future plans are not future certainties.
- Perseverance, imagination and review are vital if our vision is to be achieved.

4

I DON'T THINK IT WILL WORK

Plans and how to implement them

Plans are important, indeed essential. But for fulfilment they often require detailed decision. You may decide to relocate your office and draw up broad plans for that purpose, for example: how do you decide precisely which building to rent or buy? You plan to increase your staff, but how do you choose the precise person out of all the applicants? You may move house: how do you choose the church you want to attend? These are practical questions requiring detailed agreement to a general plan. This section describes a numerical method for reaching answers to questions like these.

Numbers and values

A *numerical* method? Tom Houston, opening a planning session at World Vision International,[1] illustrated the flippant way in which sometimes numbers are artificially linked to other considerations by describing a scene from the original film version of Martin Luther's life. The Pope in Rome was being petitioned to give the Archbishopric of Mainz to the nephew of the suitor for a fee. Ten thousand ducats were offered, 'a thousand for each of the ten commandments'.

The Pope replied, 'May I remind you there were twelve apostles.'

Responded the petitioner, 'But only seven deadly sins,' and they supposedly settled for 10,000 ducats.

Numbers can symbolise values. When Mary broke her flask

of precious perfume over Jesus just before He was crucified, Judas Iscariot said, 'It might have been sold for more than thirty silver coins and given to the poor.'[2] He measured his resentment by the value given to the flask—had it been worth only three silver coins perhaps he would not have said anything.

Our brains are exceedingly efficient, but, despite all the advanced technology and the possible gains from fifth generation computers, are still able to synthesise data by making rational and intuitive leaps which electronic imitations cannot (yet) replicate. Our decision making has to be ordered, however, and a way of doing this is to allocate numbers to values. Three examples are given below to show how this can be done and help us make decisions.

Finding your church

When we moved from Southampton to Bromley with a young family in the late 1960s, my wife and I had to find a new church. We posted identical letters to a dozen in the area on the same day so that the speed of response could be fairly compared. One minister visited us briefly on the day we moved in. 'I'm not stopping,' he said, 'I know what moving is like. But welcome to Bromley. God bless you in this house. I look forward to meeting you properly later'—and was gone. He had stayed less than two minutes.

Choose your criteria

We felt we wanted a welcoming church which had good Sunday school facilities, one where we could bring non-Christian friends, and in which we could serve in some way. It needed to be a church with which we were happy theologically and which was within reasonable distance. We then scored each out of 10 according to how important that characteristic was in our choice, as follows:

Friendliness	7
Good Sunday school	9
Helpful for non-Christians	7
Where we could serve	8

| Theological basis | 10 |
| Easy to get to | 6 |

Such numbers, technically called 'weights', effectively reflect the value we gave to each item. These may not be the criteria you would choose if you were moving. If you were handicapped you might well list as a factor the ease of physically getting into the building. If you were elderly and hard of hearing you might want to know if there was a T-loop facility to help you. It is good in this process to list as many factors as you think reasonable. None in our list scored less than 6, but it would not matter if some factors scored only 1 or 2. As George Barna said in his book *How to Find Your Church*:[3] 'If you do not know what specific characteristics and qualities you are looking for, the chances are greatly enhanced that you will not find your "ideal" church.' He urges people to be open in preparing such a list: 'Be totally honest with yourself—you don't necessarily have to share your selection criteria with other people, if you find that to be embarrassing or personal.'[4]

George Barna asked a number of people what they looked for in a church. Here are some of their criteria, which you might wish to use yourself. They chose their present church because it:

- Helped their relationship with God
- Helped their relationships with other people
- Gave real answers to tough questions
- Helped other people
- Transmitted values they appreciated
- Gave an outlet for their talents
- Was convenient to get to
- Was in the same denomination as the church they previously attended
- Held beliefs and practices they supported
- Sought to obey God.

As he also points out, there are many other criteria that could be used:[5] spiritual beliefs of the church, lifestyles of church members, the ability to make meaningful relationships within the church, the ability to have a significant worship experience, the size of the congregation, the depth of vision and quality of leadership, the programmes the church operates (Sunday school, home groups, missions projects, and so on), the location of church members vis-a-vis your home, the facilities and equipment owned by the church, and so on.

Note your comparisons

Having made your list of criteria you need also to list the various churches which you wish to assess. We listed six churches which we felt could be appropriate on the basis of replies to our letters, including the one whose minister had visited us. We knew that we were likely to be in our house for many years so we reckoned it was worth taking plenty of time to decide on our church—we took eight months.

We decided to go to each at least 3 times, after which we scored them out of 10 for each characteristic, thus:

	Weight	Church A	Church B	Church C	Church D	Church E	Church F
Friendliness	7	5	6	8	3	8	5
Good Sunday school	9	8	4	6	5	7	3
Helpful for non-Christians	7	4	5	7	2	8	4
Where we could serve	8	6	8	8	6	7	5
Theological basis	10	8	9	9	6	9	7
Easy to get to	6	9	4	10	7	9	6
Overall	47	6.7	6.2	7.9	4.9	8.0	5.0

In this process the marks given for weights are immaterial to the scores for each characteristic.

The numbers in the bottom 'overall' line, technically 'weighted averages', are calculated in the following manner. The figure at the foot of the weight column is simply the total of the six numbers above it. The figure at the foot of each church's column was calculated by multiplying the score for a particular characteristic, say friendliness, which is scored 5 for Church A,

by the weight for that characteristic, 7 in this case. 5 x 7 = 35.
This number is written down separately. Likewise the next
category is 8 x 9 = 72, the next 7 x 4 = 28, and so on. The six
numbers for each characteristic thus calculated were added
together: 35 + 72 + 28 + 48 + 80 + 54 = 317, and this total
divided by the total of the weights, 47: 317 ÷ 47 = 6.7. Likewise
for each church. As an exercise check that the score for Church
E is correct. If you do not get 8.0 look at Note 6 at the end of
the book to see what you should have done.

The results were quite clear. Two churches were well ahead
of the rest, and, as it happens, very close. As a result of this
exercise we attended Church E for three months. With experience we changed some scores, which made us feel this was not
the church we should regularly attend, so we went to Church C,
whose minister was the one who called on us, and which we
have happily attended ever since. You will notice it was not the
one with the highest score in the table above, though very close.

This whole process may be thought highly cerebral. It is. But
do not think that we were not praying that the Lord would
guide us throughout as well. We needed His wisdom to know
what scores to give to each characteristic. This may seem purely
intellectual, but these numbers reflect real values, and there is a
spiritual dimension to the scoring process.

We have spent some time on a relatively simple example to
describe the process. It is now applied to two different areas.

Moving your office

The general location

From time to time organisations have to move. Churches rarely
do, so if you are a church leader, you may wish to skip to the
next section. How do you decide where you want to move to?
Initially the question is whether to move at all from the immediate area. If your existing building is inconvenient, too small or
too out-of-date, it may be that you could move locally. You still
have to decide which property to take.

But if you are moving further afield, out of London for
example, other criteria then become relevant. It is worth drawing up a list of pros and cons, such as, for example:

A: London Location		B: Out-of-London Location	
Pros	Cons	Pros	Cons
Meeting convenience	Higher rent	Cheaper/free car parking	May be crowded
Good maintenance facilities	Higher cost of travel to work	Easy access to motorways	Smaller variety of shops and services
Specialised services nearer		Good supply of Christian part-timers	
Often quicker deliveries		Cheaper local restaurants for official entertainment	
		Some specialist suppliers near to hand	

In listing items like this it is important not to make the pros simply the positives of the cons or vice versa. Essentially list each point once in the most relevant column. If you then wish to give weights and scores to this process, fine, but usually displaying the pros and cons in this way allows the contrast between two alternatives to be more starkly realised.

The individual site

Such wider considerations help guide the basic decision of whether to choose to stay in London or go somewhere else. Whichever you choose, the process of identifying the individual site has to be worked out, and for this a detailed list comparable to those given in the previous section is required. (For those wanting such a list the proforma given on the next page may be helpful.)

It is often useful to group together similar items. If you wish you can be very precise with your scoring. For example, if you are wanting, say, 5,000 square feet of office space you might score anything of 4,000 square feet or smaller zero for size, and anything above, say 5,500 square feet 10. So if you saw something of 5,000 square feet which is two-thirds between 4,000 and

Evaluation of Alternative Properties

	Weight	Property 1	Property 2	Property 3	Property 4	Property 5
Price per square foot Size Warehousing availability						
Convenience to staff Convenience to visitors Car parking convenience						
Nearness of post office Nearness of bank Nearness of services Nearness of shops						
Image to staff Image to board/council Image to visitors						
Pleasantness of area Configuration of space Adequacy of emergency exits Ease of access with lift Adequacy of rest room/kitchen area						
Adequacy of heating Adequacy of toilets Accessibility of telephone Adequacy of computer ducting						
Does it have double glazing? Likely to be a noisy office? Adequacy of office heating Ease of cleaning offices						
Cost of business rate Cost of rent/mortgage Cost of ground rent, if any Suitable length of lease						
Possibility of subletting Gut feeling						
Other items:						
Total (Pass = 6.7)						

5,500 square feet you would score it two-thirds of 10 or 6.7. But this level of accuracy is not generally necessary.

The 'pass' score of 6.7 is a purely arbitrary figure which seems to work in practice. To have some such number gives a value to the weighted total and enables you to make a decision immediately you have seen a particular property. That speed of decision is useful. It also enables you to say, 'We have not found anything suitable yet', or, 'We have investigated twenty properties; three appear possible and one is being looked at in more detail.' This can help prayer partners, the board, staff or others with a vital interest in the decision.

This method does not tell you which property to take, but it allows you to assess a mass of different factors and emerge with a basic decision for each property—no good or possible. You then need to evaluate the 'possibles' with a finer screen and probably ask more detailed questions. The process aids guidance; it does not supplant it. It enables you to include all relevant factors, and at the degree of importance felt appropriate to each factor.

It also enables you to say why one property is better than another. Property 2 may score particularly well on, say, having a branch of your bank near. Property 4 has adequate heating, telephones and computer ducting, or whatever. This aids discussion when thinking about the relative merits of properties 2 and 4.

An example: the advantages of locating in Cambridge

The key thinking behind locations A and B is essentially one of infrastructure, and the support that gives to your work, however practical and particular the individual pros and cons may be. It would be perfectly possible to widen the discussion between A and B much further and include other considerations, and an example of this may be helpful. Cambridge has attracted many high technology firms over the last thirty years or so; why should this be? In 1960 there were 30 such firms, in 1974 100, in 1986 400 and by 1990 the number had reached 600, employing some 20,000 people, 5 per cent of all the staff in the UK employed on research and development.[7] What had caused such growth?

Cambridge is part of East Anglia, a region of small towns, close to London, with several other development areas, such as Peterborough. East Anglia's regional value of the Gross National Product (wealth indicator) is 7 per cent above the national rate, and the region has low unemployment. There are good *physical* links: the M11 motorway, the railway has been electrified, Stansted airport is being upgraded, and there is good road-port access. Telecommunications, the land, utilities and the environment are all attractive. The size of Cambridge also tells in its favour—it is small and compact, which allowed a critical mass to gather, develop and grow.

It has good *industry*, creating a skilled labour market, support services and financial skills. It has very adequate *social* benefits. There is plenty of housing, good schools, adequate parks and other recreation facilities. It is, of course, a high *intellectual* area with the university nearby, but also because of the large amount of research undertaken locally. High technology requires an information-based industry. Local *administration* is reputedly very efficient, and its future development plans wise and acceptable. For Christian people it is an area of *spiritual* growth with much church activity. The English Church Census showed Cambridgeshire was a county where the Baptists, United Reformed Church, Independent and other Free Churches were all strong and growing.[8] The Anglicans are not strongest in Cambridgeshire but are growing, and so are the Roman Catholics.

These considerations are not all. The *culture* of Cambridge is attractive for a high technological industry. The university has allowed its dons to experiment in the non-academic local commercial world, which fosters critical interaction, and provides a support and resonance of discussion opportunity which is attractive. There are some exceptional individuals in the private and public sectors who frequently meet.

Is all this sufficient? Possibly, but one major factor can be overlooked—the *personal* factor. One particular local bank in Cambridge has had a succession of especially high quality managers with an imaginative innovative approach which has backed risks and has seen many winners as a consequence. Of the 600 high technology firms within a ten-mile radius of

Cambridge in 1990, 54 per cent were new companies, not expansions of existing enterprises. That kind of growth happens when high calibre people are involved. Often people are the major factor.

Choosing your people

Your staff

The same broad principles relating to moving your office can apply to selecting your staff—be they part time or full time, lay or ordained, male or female, paid or volunteer. This is not a guide on how to interview candidates, but a way of evaluating all the many aspects from their interviews. Before advertising any post you need to draw up a job description. (How to go about this from a Christian perspective is given in Eddie Gibbs's excellent book *Followed or Pushed?*[9])

Many employers have found that a simple interview is not always sufficient for a thorough appraisal of a candidate and also use various skill, aptitude and personality tests. At MARC Europe we use such tests to give an indication of candidates' administrative skills, team building ability, initiative and decision-making qualities. We also seek to assess practically their professional skills—secretaries will be asked to do a keyboard test, research assistants a presentation demonstrating their analytical skills, for example. We also sometimes ask candidates to prepare for a presentation at the time of interview. There is much detail to evaluate from all these procedures.

A list of categories for personnel interviewing that MARC Europe uses for secretaries, and which churches or organisations may find useful, follows.

Evaluation of Secretary

	Weight	Person 1	Person 2	Person 3	Person 4	Person 5
Pleasantness of personality	10					
Pleasantness of physical appearance	9					
Clarity of speech	9					
Helpful telephone manner	9					
Experience—filing systems	7					
—audio typing	10					
—word processing	10					
—information retrieval	7					
—desk research	9					
—volume of mail	8					
Quickness of uptake	10					
Good reasoning powers	8					
Reliability under pressure	10					
Likely perseverance	10					
Likely potential	5					
Likely motivation	8					
Thoroughness in detail	10					
Likely to show initiative	10					
Likely adaptability	9					
Acceptance of responsibility	10					
Likely to get on with others	10					
Willingness to tackle anything	10					
Good sense of publicity	7					
Numerical ability	5					
Good organiser of others	10					
Organised themselves	10					
Administrative experience	8					
Management experience	5					
Likely loyalty	7					
State of health	8					
Likely reaction to stress	10					
Apparent spirituality	10					
Test 1—writing problem-solving letter	10					
Test 2—self-evaluation of personal strengths	8					
Test 3—keyboard test	10					
Test 4—organising typical task	8					
Others (to be added as necessary)						
TOTAL (Pass = 6.7)	314					

Other categories are added for other positions. For research assistants, for instance, we add experience on a computer, collecting information, report writing, involvement in research. We need to consider their adaptability, their maturity, knowledge of statistical theory. So we test them on numeracy, personality and administration.

We retain the pass score of 6.7 and rarely appoint someone scoring less than 7.0; most are in the range 7.3 to 7.8. Only three times have we appointed people scoring between 6.7 and 7.0, and all three proved unsuitable. If this kind of evaluation works for one organisation, it is likely to work for others. It obviously can be adapted to include whatever characteristics are felt desirable in churches, other charities or firms.

Your board

Choosing people is not confined only to staff, of course. Many Christian organisations have a board or council or general committee whose members have to be appointed. Churches have elders, deacons or the Parochial Church Council. How does one best find them? It is worth asking what kind of board you want? What do you expect of them? Do they act as a council of reference lending their name? Do they act as a group responsible for policy while the general secretary is responsible for leadership? Do they act as a management group with responsibility for many of the detailed decisions? Whom you select depends on the answers to questions like these. These answers are, in effect, a kind of job description for your members, much less detailed than for staff, but still worth spelling out in a letter when approaching someone to serve in such a position.

Some organisations try to reflect on their council skills and experience matching the key types of operation in which they are involved. An organisation working much in the Third World, for example, can usefully have expatriates or missionaries who have worked in such countries. Some organisations with specialist opportunities need competent technical advisers. Those with many staff might find a personnel officer useful. Most have financial needs, which perhaps explains why so many Christian accountants get requests to serve on councils! Drawing up a list of suitable skills can help. Include in the list some of the key geographical areas in which you work also. What balance do you need between the genders? (Should the board of governors in a girls' school, for example, have a majority of women on it?) What age bands do you want reflected on your governing body? If you have too many elderly people will you have enough energy for movement? If you have too many young people will you have sufficient wisdom and experience?

Since a specific example so often aids clarity, we give below the form used at one stage for MARC Europe's board.

Board Members

	Person A	Person B	Person C	Person D	Person E	Person F	Person G	Person H
Christian researcher								
Statistician								
Publisher								
Marketing specialist								
Communicator								
General manager								
Administrator								
With financial acumen								
Church statesman								
Missiologist								
Nationality: British								
Finnish								
German								
American								
Male								
Female								
Under 40								
Over 40								

This allows some of the talents and circumstances of past or present board members to be readily seen. If MARC Europe wished to expand its board, what type of person should be considered? Where are the gaps? This kind of analysis is easy, concentrates the mind wonderfully, and helps movement into the direction of meeting needs felt within the organisation. 'Without counsel plans go wrong, but with many advisers they succeed.'[10] A good council or church leadership team is essential for effectiveness.

The above examples show how decision making can be aided through the use of straightforward planning grids where numbers reflect the values of assessments made. 'The plans of the diligent,' says Proverbs again, 'lead surely to abundance.'[11]

Avoiding bureaucratic cramp

We may introduce planning to our church or organisation. We may simplify decision-making procedures, but ultimately we must avoid letting the bureaucracy we can so easily create stop us actually doing the job. It is said that a good gardener always plants three seeds—one for the grubs, one for the weather and one for himself.[12] His style is not cramped by bureaucratic logic.

Robert Horton, chairman of BP, is thinking of flexibility (avoiding cramp) when he says, 'In the 1980s we learned to manage change. In the 1990s we shall need to learn to manage surprise.'[13] Bernard O'Keefe, who leads an American high technology business firm, says, 'Planning systems are inherently risk averse. They cannot give you the inspiration that tells you where you go next.'[14] Precisely so! Plans and systems are crucial and important but ultimately it is your vision which will be the dynamic of your organisation, not the bureaucratic processes by which it is run. 'The final act of an institution,' Cicero wrote in AD 31, 'is to write down its rules and regulations.' An organisation cannot afford to be chained to the past.

IBM uses its planning system for communication, not control,[15] and so should we. The plan is a process.

> We talk to each other by plan. I have a sheet here, and the top line on it is the plan and its status. You can go to a product manager and say 'How's business?' Within the

first four sentences he or she will tell you how things are going compared to the plan. The same thing happens if you go to a territory representative at IBM—how things are going versus quota. So we use the plan all the time to communicate formally and informally with each other.[16]

The plan is a guide; flexibility in following it is essential.

Charles Inge encapsulated this thought in a verse of doggerel, the theology of which needs strengthening:

> This very remarkable man
> Commends a most remarkable plan:
> You can do what you want
> If you don't think you can't,
> So don't think you can't think you can.

What then is flexibility with respect to planning? It is illustrated by a charter airline's analysis of its time keeping on a particular flight. It had a remarkable record of being within two minutes of its estimated time of arrival on 94 per cent of the flights, despite the pilot making significant variations from his registered flight plan in 92 per cent of the 'on time' flights. Yet he achieved his target. All kinds of events had intervened: wind speed changed, wind direction altered, heavy traffic meant diversions, and so on. Yet by trimming his rudder, changing his speed and rerouting in mid-air he could still achieve his plan.[17] A church or organisation is like those aircraft—adjust according to circumstances but seek to fulfil your plan still.

Summary

- Numbers can sometimes usefully symbolise values.
- Making a decision depends on many factors needing careful assessment.
- Moving your office requires evaluation of many factors.
- Choosing the right people for your staff or board is critical, and attention to both impressions and facts vital.
- Predetermined plans should never exclude inspiration and initiative.

5

I DON'T HAVE TIME TO ANSWER THAT

Paperwork and how to beat it

How you view the time you have is critical to its use. 'Remember,' said the American statesman Benjamin Franklin, 'time is money.' This is the *economic* view. A simple calculation can show how much you are paid per hour and so how much it could be said to cost to, say, meet someone or spend thirty minutes writing a letter.

The C.S. Lewis comment mentioned earlier ('Christians often seem to have a lot of time; you may wonder where it comes from') reflects the *pastoral* view. Time spent with friends, or comforting the bereaved, or counselling an aching heart is rarely measured by the minute. We give to others because the need is there, and we share the benefits of the fellowship or help this gives.

'On my calendar,' wrote Martin Luther, 'There are but two days: today, and That Day.' The *eternal* view weighs up time used against the final judgement. Part of the condemnation of the servant who received just one talent and buried it in the ground is the laziness implied in such action—he did not think of his actions in the light of the reckoning to come.

The American politican, Adlai Stevenson, commented that 'in the long run, it is not the years in your life but the life in your years that counts'. The *quality* view is linked to both the pastoral and eternal view, but reflects the totality of what we do, and the value of it. It reflects, too, the importance of being satisfied with what you have done. When God created the world

He took six days over it. At the end of each day, except the second, He 'saw that it was good'.[1] He was content with what had been accomplished; and so should we. After making the sun, moon and stars on the third day, God did not say, 'Bother, I haven't created the birds and the fish.' That was His fourth day's work. We need to be encouraged by the tasks accomplished, not daunted by the labours yet to come.

Lewis Carroll reflects a *personal* view of time as a daily companion to be treated with respect, wisdom, and kindliness:

> Alice sighed heavily. 'I think you might do something better with time,' she said, 'than wasting it asking riddles with no answers.'
> 'If you knew Time as well as I do,' said the Hatter. 'You wouldn't talk about wasting *it*. It's *him*.'

Have we treated our hours this day sensibly or have we taken advantage of them unfairly and wasted them—abused the relationship, as it were?

These various views of time epitomise how we handle our paperwork. It costs money to type a letter. Letters are an essential part of our pastoral ministry. We can never neglect the eternal. The quality of our life is more than paperwork, which yet yields personal satisfaction when well done.

Fighting for time

The constant need to control our time is underlined by Peter Drucker, the guru of much modern management thinking. 'Nothing so distinguishes effective executives,' he says, 'as much as their tender loving care of time.' This is never so true when it comes to paperwork.

How do you take tender, loving care of your time spent dealing with paperwork, the bane of most leaders, executives and others? That care is epitomised by a determination to make your time count, and therefore to squeeze out the myriad of time wasters.

A friend noticed that a visitor coming to his house took off his jacket simultaneously with his anorak. When he asked why, he was told, 'It all saves time.' Good time management makes this paraphrase of the old proverb, 'Take care of the minutes and the hours take care of themselves.' We have to fight for our time especially when we handle paper. Surgeons bend over the patient on the operating table. 'How's it going?' you may ask. 'Another hour and we'll be there.' Their fight for life and health is measured by time.

The battle for our time is nowhere more urgent than in the paperwork which floods so many desks. With the rise of unsolicited 'direct' mail we seem besieged and the postman's visit is dreaded rather than welcomed. Of all mail in the USA, 14 per cent was 'direct' mail in 1945; in 1989 it was 39 per cent.[2] A similar rise has occurred in Britain: the average UK home received more than one piece of direct mail per week in 1990. Fax machines make the paper war more urgent. They deliver their piece of scrolled paper with the implicit cry 'Now!' In 1988 3 per cent of Christian organisations had a fax machine; three years later the *UK Christian Handbook* showed it had risen to 26 per cent.

Electronic mail crowds our word processing screens if we are connected to such a system; many irrelevant messages have to be scanned as well as the serious ones—how truly effective are they in communicating? I sometimes wonder. They give us speed in communication but not always a true indication of its value.

Mastering the volume of paperwork

Two men by a desk piled several feet high with paper are looking for their secretary. 'She must be here somewhere,' says one, 'I hear sobbing!' Paperwork can so easily submerge us (if not quite so literally). Once I had to visit a senior civil servant in Edinburgh. His desk, his side table, his filing cabinet, his book-case, his cupboard, the table in the middle of his room, and several chairs were all totally covered by papers eighteen inches high. 'Sit down,' he said, so I did by a chair the other side of his desk. He literally had to move two mounds of paper apart to see me as we talked!

Your paperwork may be nowhere near as bad as that but you may still have to control it. A Bible Society survey in 1980 showed that Anglican clergy receive approximately twice as much mail as Free Church ministers.[3] So much for the joy of belonging to the state church! One diocesan bishop recently said he received on average fifty items of mail a day.

This chapter shows a way through this paper jungle, and gives a method for handling paperwork, controlling filing, and monitoring future activities.

Correspondence and other items requiring attention

The key to successful handling of correspondence and other paperwork is at heart simple—have a system and follow the golden rule.

The golden rule

> Handle each piece of paper as few times as possible and preferably just once.

'As few times as possible' means minimising the times paper moves from the in tray to a pending tray, or from the pending tray back to the in tray, or from 'brief-up' (explained later but meaning papers received in the past which relate to present activities) and back again. I do not use a pending tray, finding it just another source of paper awaiting action. I prefer to deal decisively with my in tray, with any items requiring future action assigned to brief-up. All items requiring present decision wait in my in tray.

It also means not reading my correspondence in detail when received; it is scanned, of course, to know into what pile it goes. Three minutes reading each of ten letters a day takes thirty minutes, most of which will have to be repeated when I reply.

'As few times as possible' means assigning each incoming piece of paper to a specific category and keeping it there until it is dealt with. The pressure for action then comes on all the items in a particular category, and if the categories are prioritised this automatically means the most urgent are handled first.

Categories of paperwork

The categories used for sorting paperwork vary with the person and the nature of the work. In the award winning Rank Xerox film *Time to Think* a manager is shown using four categories: action, information, reading and WPB (waste paper basket). If these four work for you, fine, use them. If you need more detail, have more detail. Some find six categories useful. Do not have too many, however—eight is almost certainly a maximum for ease of use.

I find the following six useful:

> External mail
> Internal mail
> Reading material
> Invoices
> Messages
> Brief-up.

Make up and label plastic files or card folders, or other containers for each category. As post is opened and sorted, it should immediately be put into one of them. If for some reason they are not cleared one day, the following day's letters should be put underneath in the same folder. If your work pattern is to take one such pile of folders and work through them, have a second set for your secretary to use while you work with the first.

External mail. This is mail which comes from outside your church or organisation. It relates to your outside audience or market. It should include personal mail sent to your office rather than your home. (Mail from your diocese, your superintendent, your national headquarters counts as internal mail.) External mail comes from individuals requiring information, advice or guidance. It includes those who write impersonally to your organisation ('The Incumbent', 'The Editor' or 'The Director', or whoever). It includes those replying to your letters asking for details or help.

Internal mail relates to your team ministry, reflecting your ongoing pastoral communication and support work. It comes from various sources. If you work in a church or organisation, this item will include internal memos, or the note your church secretary hands you on Sunday morning. It may come electronically via E-mail (almost, by definition, this is limited to insiders, or at least users of your network) or via the postal service. 'Internal' simply denotes the source, not whether the communication is urgent or non-urgent, confidential or open.

There are advantages of classifying mail into these two groups. You can tell at a glance which predominates. If 95 per cent of your mail as a Christian leader is internal, for example, what does that say about your ministry? For a minister it may be appropriate, but not for a departmental head.

The classification into external and internal also allows you to reflect the priority you give them. Your handling of external mail helps to give your church or organisation its *image*. (When we were looking for a church the speed of response gave one indication of the quality or efficiency of its leader.) Your internal mail reflects on your *responsibilities*. If you feel your image is more important, answer your external mail first.

Reading material. This obviously includes books, magazines, papers, and perhaps the occasional cassette or video. The first question to ask about any reading material is 'Does it have to be read today?' Very rarely is the answer 'Yes', but when it is, decide then exactly when to read it—immediately, or after lunch, or over a cup of tea mid-afternoon. Allocate a time of action when you handle the item—reading materials too need to be handled as few times as possible so don't think 'it will be good to read that sometime today'; decide when at the time of looking at it.

I find reading material can be put into three broad categories (after any immediate is taken out):

- The ephemeral. This relates to magazine articles, newsletters, reports, extended items of information, publicity brochures, journals, and so on. I like to try to clear my pile of these once a week if possible. Some of it is important for action, so it then moves to my external or internal mail categories as appropriate. Some of it requires prayer, so it moves to an alphabetical prayer file, in which everything is prayed for at least three times in the next three months. Some of it can be thrown away; other items must be kept for reference. Some needs to be passed on to others to scan and retain or scrap.

This is the pile from which I take material when travelling. Here is reading material which can be looked at if there is time before an appointment, or in a train or if traffic is held up; something which can pass minutes or, if necessary, an hour or two. We are fighting for time. Always take some time-fillers in case you are caught unexpectedly with minutes in hand. It saves those minutes later on.

What if the pile gets too high for ready clearing by such means? It may well become a sufficient priority for you to allocate regular reading time specifically for that purpose: say, two hours on a particular weekday. When adding to the pile put more urgent items above the less urgent. Some mail might be thrown away rather than added to the pile.

- The necessary. These are books, reports and other major items of reading which you need to read for your work. They are anything which is essential for you to know, to learn, to understand for your responsibilities to be better fulfilled. How often this pile needs to be cleared will vary with the individual. I put no time limit on them but never put them on to any bookshelves until read. The Bishop of Warrington, Michael Henshall, goes away twice each year for a 'reading week' to tackle this pile. Others assign fewer days but more frequently for the same purpose.
- The desirable. These are books, papers or reports which you want, as opposed to feel you have, to read. They might be detective stories, serious works of theology or anything in between. I find it a good motivation to promise myself a book from this pile after reading one from the previous pile (except on holiday when I read only desirable books).

Other types of paperwork

These will vary from person to person.

Invoices. Perhaps you have to approve all expenditure in your church, or sign cheques, or every large cheque in your organisation. Deal with these once a week, or twice a month, as appropriate. Grouping things together aids speed in handling, and often allows comparisons to be made in expenditure which might be missed if taken intermittently.

Messages. These include telephone calls taken in your absence when there is no answering machine. These are often urgent, and should be handled as soon as convenient. They are originated in a personal way—a spoken communication, not a piece of paper—and following the priority of God-People-Work should take precedence over other items. Your image of efficiency is also furthered in one small way, quite apart from the call of courtesy.

Fax items can often be treated as post, but some are urgent (for example, checking proofs of artwork) and should be treated as messages.

Brief-up. This should be treated either as internal mail and handled accordingly, or put as reading (perhaps it's material required for a meeting you have next week sent several weeks ago), or give it a new brief-up date. This is defined and explained in more detail below.

Answering external and internal mail

To keep the golden rule of handling pieces of paper as few times as possible, and preferably just once, you must use a system. This has been described for other categories of paper, but not mail. External and internail mail may be treated in the same manner. All mail may be handled by answering three questions:

Does it have to be answered? Yes. How quickly should you answer? There are only two variations—short term and medium term. Short term may be defined as today or within forty-eight hours, medium term as this week or within ten calendar days. If you have no secretary, or only a part-time typist to help you, such periods may be too short. Then define short term as within three days and medium term as within two weeks. But do not make your medium term longer.

Note there is no long term. To take longer than, say, two weeks to reply to a letter is discourteous, gives a poor image and may make the sender wonder whether you have received it and write again, creating more, and unnecessary, paperwork. If you do take longer than two weeks to reply, apologise. It sometimes helps to note when a letter is received, as this can vary considerably from the date on the letter, especially one from overseas.

A letter arrives asking you to speak at a convention in eighteen months' time; another from a student asks you for a reading list of books on Christian leadership, and a third from a church member reveals that his family needs special help. How do you deal with these?

The family that needs help requires answering immediately. Depending on the nature of the help, you may choose to phone or visit instead. The convention invitation can be quickly dealt with by checking whether or not the date is convenient, but you may also need to make further inquiries about the organisers, or pray over it first, so it becomes a medium term answer.

If it is not possible to produce the reading list immediately, give a short-term answer saying that you will be glad to provide it in, say, the next four weeks. This does several things: it is courteous, and shows you have received the letter, reflecting well on your image and efficiency. You have also indicated your timetable for providing the information. If this is inconvenient to the recipient, he can ask if you could manage it earlier, explaining why. You can then reschedule or not as you are able, but then your action and your reply are based on open know ledge and understanding of what each is doing and requiring. That can only aid effectiveness and time management.

This sequence may be shown thus:

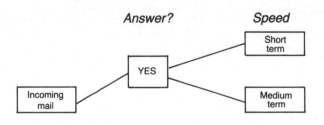

Is further action required? When an answer is given, what do you do with the original and your copy of the reply? If no further action is required file the letter away. A filing cabinet is not a pending tray, so put nothing in it which requires future actions. If further action will be necessary, put the letter in brief-up, which is for precisely that purpose—a collection of papers on which action must one day be taken.

If the family needing help requires counselling put their letter and your reply in brief-up in time for that first appointment if more than a day or two away. The student's reading list, once compiled, requires no further action, but you may wish to file it for future reference in case anyone else asks something similar. The convention engagement requires no immediate further action after you have accepted it (assuming you do), but you will need to read up on the subject and prepare your talk or message well in time, so put it into brief-up for, say, fifteen months' time to allow you three months for preparation next year. The sequence is thus:

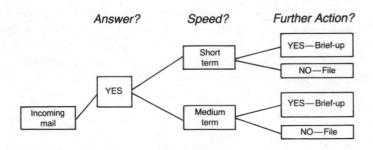

How many copies should be made of a reply? This partly depends on your organisation, but the answer will usually be one or two. Only make no copy at all if it does not matter to you whether the letter arrives or not (notification of a change of address for example—if your letter does not arrive you will find out next time you send something). Make a single copy, to go into your file, only if it contains little substance (a thanks for a service rendered, for example. You may want to know later that you acknowledged help, but nothing more). If it is of substance, make two copies, one for filing by topic, the other for a 'time file' with all your correspondence in date order. A time file provides an ordered source for tracing the letter. I have often found mine useful. ('That came up last May. Look in the time file to see if we replied then.') As Robert Orben wrote in *The Wall Street Journal*, 'Noah had to be the first bureaucrat. He filed two of everything.'[4]

With many letters typed on word processors, with consequent storage of content on disks, a policy of how many of these to retain will need to be worked through, and the number, if any, of other back-up copies. For transient correspondence it may well not be worth retaining at all, except for making a back-up copy of current memory, with perhaps an annual weeding-out exercise. It can easily take longer searching for the appropriate item on a disk than retyping from a photostat copy.

Occasionally you may wish to write your answer on an original letter and return it to the sender. This does not create a good image, but it is quick and convenient. It is worth using where speed is important, substance light, and your recipient well known to you.

This would add to the sequence as follows (using dotted lines to show this is an irregular and only occasional route):

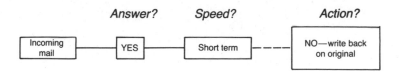

Does it have to be answered? No. If you do not answer a letter write 'no answer' and the date on it so you will know later how you dealt with it. That saves searching for a reply which subsequently you may think had been sent! A few seconds to write 'no answer' may save an hour in two months' time.

The letter not needing an answer may simply be one of thanks—you may wish to file it. It may be a brief cover of material you will need to go through to prepare that convention talk next year. The enclosures you may decide to put into your 'necessary reading' file. The letter may be a subscription order form, tax reminder, or a note that someone's twenty-fifth anniversary or birthday is next November. Put that into brief-up. Or it may simply be a piece that you have no need to keep, so throw it away.

The sequence thus is:

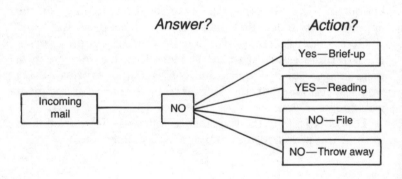

This process thus gives you a sequence of operations to follow with both external and internal mail. Having established that process, it is important to keep to it. There is no point in devising a system for the more efficient handling of your paperwork and then not using it! The whole sequence is combined opposite.

Handling External or Internal Mail

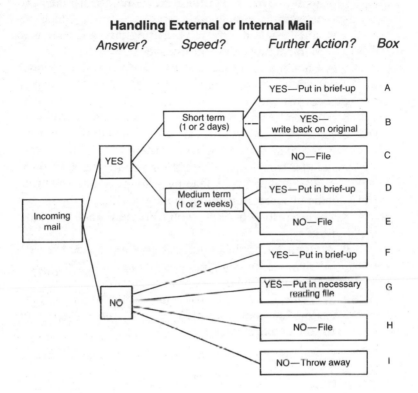

| *Answer?* | *Speed?* | *Further Action?* | *Box* |

How does it work in practice?

Test yourself. Into which of the further action categories in the above diagram would you put the following pieces of correspondence?

1 A request to help funding an expensive project which bears little relation to the work of your church or organisation.

2 A letter from the local radio station asking for details of your activities over the next six months so they can request interviews in good time.

3 A note from an old friend inviting you and your wife for a meal on Friday in three weeks' time.

4 A pleading request for advice for a member of your church whose daughter has become totally deaf after recovering from meningitis.

5 A brochure advertising next year's special diary.

6 A letter asking you to explain the meaning of a paragraph in an article you had written for your magazine.

7 A letter from a colleague asking you to help at the next quarterly meeting by leading a discussion on the problems of successful church management.

8 An interesting book for you to review when you have time.

9 A circular from headquarters giving proposed revised instructions for completing your annual return, due in eight months' time.

10 A memo from your boss/bishop/superintendent/moderator/chairman asking for your outline programme for the coming year.

Suggested answers may be found in Note 5 at the end of the book.

The two terms frequently used above—filing and brief-up—are now looked at in more detail.

Filing systems

What should a filing system be used for? What kind of system is the most efficient? The key statement is:

> The purpose of a filing system is to allow something to be retrieved, not stored.

If you wish to store papers, material, reports you no longer regularly use, put them in your archives, library, basement, attic, church hall, downstairs cupboard or wherever, but do not leave them in your filing cabinet! A filing cabinet should contain the papers you need for your current work, and should allow easy access to them. Papers packed tight in a drawer are never easy to get out.

Thus we have the space for a system to operate, and avoid the difficulty depicted below:

Fig 13: 'Well, I know it was here last May!'

Key principles

We have all lost a letter and searched for it endlessly, only to find it in the last place we think of looking. But our fight for time must be just as real in retrieving papers required for today's work. How can we ensure we can find what we want? The following methods are important:

Use small discrete categories rather than large general ones. Do not have 'general', 'miscellaneous' or 'other papers' files. It is so easy to make these inches thick and still never find the paper we urgently require. Use no label such as 'The World'! Instead use small precise categories. As a guiding rule no file should be more than three-quarters of an inch thick. When it gets to that size split it into two.

Use the same material and labelling for all your files. It makes handling much easier if you constantly use the same type of file for all your material, whether this is plastic, wallet, thin card, suspended or not, vertical or horizontal, A4 or foolscap, and so on. We find using horizontal filing in four-drawer cabinets, with papers in each file kept in a card folder, labelled also with the file number, the most suitable. We can then remove the whole file by taking out the card folder. Particular groups of paper within an individual file are kept together in plastic files. Label all files boldly.

Keep the files in a logical order. It does not matter whether this is numerical, alphabetical, chronological, or any other order, so long as it is rational and relevant and obvious to other users. It is sometimes worth making the numerical references meaningful.

Keep a numerical list of file headings. It is much easier to flick through a list of headings to decide on an appropriate number for a new project than scan through the drawers of a cabinet. This is best kept in a loose-leaf folder so that extra pages can be added. Leave plenty of space between headings for later additions.

Also keep an alphabetical index. A reference number is useful only if it can be found quickly; an alphabetical list allows this. Again make it loose leaf, labelling twenty-six sheets A to Z.

The alphabetical list can be augmented by indexing *subjects*. If you have a lot of papers on, say, urban mission, or women in ministry, or French churches, index them as appropriate. Index also by *author*. Are the writings of C.S. Lewis useful? Then list Lewis, C.S. (list people under their surname however well known their Christian name may be: thus Billy Graham would be under G, not B). Sometimes the *source* is useful. The organisation Pro Mundi Vita produced at one stage a most useful list of research monographs, so we listed these under P. When helpful, index the *key word* of the title. An article, 'Young People in Urban Mission', might be kept in your urban mission file, but index additionally under Y (young people) to give the necessary cross-reference.

Does all this not take time? Yes it does, but we are fighting for time, trying to make more effective use of our time, and being able to find facts, correspondence, books, articles quickly as necessary saves time (and much frustration) in the long run. Today there are also available any number of simple database software packages for use on your personal computer.

Individual systems

Gordon MacDonald, a popular preacher, uses 'tomato' files, an idea he gleaned from watching his wife once plant tomato seeds: lots of little seeds all put carefully in particular places.[6] He created a lot of little files into which he puts ideas, illustrations for sermons or talks, notes, and so on, which may be of future use.

Canon Michael Saward has been marketing for nearly thirty years a filing system specifically relevant to church leaders, covering all aspects of a minister's work. Primarily designed for Anglican clergy (one in eight of whom use it), it is sufficiently broad and flexible to be useful to those in other denominations. There are eight major subdivisions, and then further subdivisions within each of these, and the subdivisions can be broken down further if necessary. He also provides a detailed index. The major sections of his system are listed in Appendix 4 for illustration, together with two subdivisions.

Regularly discard unwanted paper

For the first two working days of every year MARC Europe is closed for stocktaking, which we genuinely do. We also spend time clearing out all our filing cabinets, word processor storage space, computer memories, boxes of papers, books, and so on. All the correspondence for the past year is gone through, and the non-essentials thrown out. All spare copies are thrown away. The library is checked for surplus material, electronic memories reduced. We make a game of it: the staff wear old clothes, and someone goes out for doughnuts mid-morning. Our purpose is serious, though—to get rid of all the paper we no longer need, and especially to prune the many files in our filing cabinets. No one is allowed more than one four-drawer filing cabinet. We thus make space for development for the year ahead. Our example, publicised in our 'Effective Use of Time' seminar, has inspired others to follow suit.

A 'brief-up' system

A brief-up (B/U) system can be called by various names, such as 'reminder system' or 'bring forward', but its basic function is the same.

> The purpose of a brief-up system is to call to mind future actions logically by date order.

That is to say, it brings together into one chronological sequence for your attention at the appropriate future time all the various papers which affect your work.

Uses of a brief-up system

The following types of material are particularly suitable for a brief-up system.

Papers for forthcoming meetings and conferences. This may include reading material, travel directions, rail tickets, a conference programme, and so on.

Correspondence needing additional or future action. There are times when you need to follow up promises made ('I'll send you details of that meeting when the programme is finalised'), to check up on actions ('Did you send off the insurance form, churchwarden?'), to ensure your counsel is used ('What did you decide to do, then?'), to take advantage of future meetings ('Good to see you at this fraternal. I've been asked to speak at the annual conference this year. What line do you think I should take?'), or to collect data ('Next Sunday is the day we have to count how many come. How do you suggest we can best do that?').

Reminders to prepare talks, or arrange journeys. It can also be useful to ensure you don't forget your wedding anniversary!

Check papers or projects. A good manager controls and monitors developments. It does not need to be heavy handed, but a gentle reminder can work wonders: 'How's that new Sunday school programme getting on?', or 'What did the superintendent say about the mission scheme?'

Reminders to contact people. Before you can check that the insurance form was sent out you may need to contact the person concerned in the first place!

How it works

To operate such a system, *write B/U and the date* in, say, the top right corner of each appropriate piece of paper (the actual position is less important than consistency of location).

Then *file these papers* in chronological order. Special files labelled '1–31' for the days of the month, and 'Jan–Dec' are available, but a couple of files in a drawer of a filing cabinet are generally quite sufficient—one for the current month, and one for the rest.

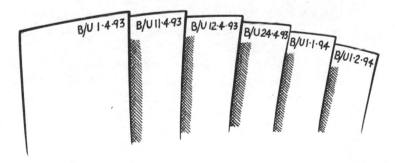

Fig 14: File brief-up papers in date order

Check your brief-up file each day. Some write the necessary details in their diaries, and some current time-planner diaries allow for this. It just needs to become a habit for you or your secretary.

Helping people be efficient

A well-known Christian leader spoke at an evangelism strategy meeting. 'I'm not sure I should have come to this conference,' he said, 'I've left papers all over my desk.' It is important to organise our paperwork but we must never let it rule us.

Tom Peters, in his book *Thriving on Chaos*, pleads with leaders and managers to be involved with people:

> Vigorously, gleefully, with all hands participating, take the lead in destroying the trappings of bureaucracy. Tear up papers. Refuse to read them. Be outrageous. Get rid of all your filing cabinets. Put big cardboard boxes around your desk and throw all the junk you receive into them— unread. Put a big red label on the boxes: 'This week's unread paperwork.' Be colourful. Have a Friday after-noon ceremony, once a month at 4 pm. Bring beer and invite your people to the incinerator. Burn all the paper you received but did not read. You've got two choices: find your own style of doing this, or go broke.[7]

In our fight for time we must keep paperwork in perspective. Sir John Lubbock gives good advice: 'If we are in doubt what to do, it is a good rule to ask ourselves what we shall wish on the morrow that we had done.'[8]

Two men chopped wood all day long. One worked straight through, without stopping to rest. At the end of the day he had a sizable pile of logs. The other would chop for fifty minutes and then take a ten-minute break. At the end of the day he had a much larger pile.

'How could you chop more?' asked the man who had worked continuously.

His friend replied, 'When I stopped for a rest, I also sharp-ened my axe.'[9]

Planning our paperwork is equivalent to sharpening our axe.

Summary

- How we view our time is critical to its use.
- We have to fight for effective use of our time.
- Handle each piece of paper as few times as possible and preferably just once.
- Categorise your mail. Does it have to be answered? If yes, how quickly? Any further action required?
- The purpose of a filing system is to allow something to be retrieved, not stored.
- Annually weed out unwanted paper and create space for current work.
- The purpose of a brief-up system is to calendarise logically future actions.
- Rule your paperwork. Do not let it rule you.

6

I DON'T HAVE TIME TO DO THAT NOW

Tools for Time Management

The fight for time is not confined to paperwork, though that is a good place to start. If we are serious we have to take that fight into other key areas, especially those often labelled 'administration'. Speaking for an hour on time management to a group of theological college students one day, I was told, 'That is the only hour we've spent on this subject in our four years at college!' Surveys show church leaders spend up to half their time on administration, with most disliking it, and many having had no training in it.

A survey of 800 church leaders, gathered for a national event, asked what was their biggest problem.[1] 'Lack of time and too much work,' they answered. What was the most important thing a Christian leader should do? 'Personal prayer,' two-thirds replied. 'Administration' was ticked by only 5 per cent. What do ministers most enjoy doing? 'Praise and worship,' half replied. Only 3 per cent said, 'Administration'. What takes most of your time, they were asked. The foremost item?— 'administration'! So we have the situation where many clergy dislike administration, do not regard it as important, but have to spend much of their time doing it! That is a sure recipe for nagging frustration, high pressure, and unrelieved stress. Lest that survey be thought exceptional, others have subsequently revealed exactly the same findings.[2]

Part of the problem is the habits we have. The saying 'Old habits die hard' is never so true as in the area of organisation.

Mark Twain might be paraphrased, 'Habits can't be flung out of the window, they have to be coaxed downstairs, a step at a time.'[3] Most habits in churches are as difficult to break as for individuals. 'We've never done it this way before' are sometimes rightly called the seven last words of a church.

In physics, entropy means a measure of the disorder in a closed system. From this comes the second law of thermodynamics—everything that is organised will break down or run down unless it is maintained.

> Examples of entropy's workings can be found throughout the everyday world. Desks will get messy. Cars will wear out. Stars will blow up. Without librarians, books get scattered and jumbled. Lacking nutrients, organisms die and rot. In each case, a highly organised system will initially proceed to a state of disorder and chaos unless energy [which is equivalent to work] is brought into the system to re-establish order.[4]

Whatever else fighting is about, it is about using energy. If we are determined to win more time for the things we must do, things we need to do to fulfil our goals and vision, things we want to do because we enjoy doing them, then we have to win precious minutes and hours in every aspect of our day-by-day living. This chapter looks at ten key areas and shows how our administration can become more efficient.

Organising your diary

In this section we mean by 'diary' that schedule of meetings, appointments, notes of action, and so on, that are essential for daily work, not as Pepys used the term, otherwise called a journal. A journal notes your private and personal thoughts; a diary public and presentable happenings.

Diaries are essential for work for most Western people, organisations and churches. We need to use them efficiently, however, if we are to save precious time by eliminating things we should not be doing; doing what we should be doing more efficiently; and doing the more important things first.

There are many types of diary on the market. Filofax is one of the most well known and is regularly used by millions. Tempus is a specifically Christian type of Filofax, that is to say, a ring binder larger than Filofax with preprinted pages for diary and for other areas of work which ministers undertake. Day-Timers (UK) Ltd produce a loose-leaf diary, also with many preprinted pages. Filofax have introduced Deskfax, a larger desk-sized edition with nine rings rather than the more familiar hand-sized version with six rings. W.H. Smith market their own form of diary, and numerous other brands are available. If you are satisfied with your diary do not change it, but if not, find one which suits your needs. (Some years ago I found myself frustrated with my diary simply because I could not buy the next year's diary before June or July. I needed one earlier than that, and, discovering Filofax was available in March, switched to that. They also do blank diary pages for those really keen to mark up their year very early!)

Electronic diary packages are now readily available in a wide variety of forms, as well as portable personal organisers with quick reference facilities.

Control of your diary

Who should keep your diary? Those with a personal assistant or secretary often find it helpful to let her make all their appointments, but then should never make commitments without consulting her. If you travel a lot, or are likely to make new appointments or arrange further meetings wherever you are, it is probably less frustrating for you personally to be in charge of your diary. Your secretary should then always say to an enquirer that she must confirm your availability with you. There must be only one final arbiter of what goes into a diary, however. If you both make definite bookings you have a sure recipe for frustration.

One diary or two?

How far should you integrate your personal diary with your work diary? Your evening appointments, meeting with friends, family gatherings, holidays and relaxation times, and so on, are part of your personal life. Some prefer to keep these apart from a work diary since these mostly relate to evenings and weekends and work mostly relates to events during the day. But they can overlap with late afternoon appointments and create timing problems. Personally I prefer to have one single system on which everything is recorded and in order, like the nicely balanced taste from mixing meat and onions on a kebab skewer. Others operate a dual system. If your present system leads to conflict of engagements and cancellation of appointments, or frequent changes of times to meet, it suggests that your system is inefficient and integrating the two might help. Ultimately the way you work is up to you because your diary is precisely that— *your* diary.

Sharing your diary

Whoever keeps your diary, and whether your diary includes personal and work events or not, invariably other people need to know broadly what you are doing. Colleagues need to know whether they can reach you at certain times, your spouse needs to know if you will be out or away on particular evenings, people need to know where to contact you in an emergency. So finding a means of sharing your diary is important, in outline, not in detail.

Planners showing a whole year at once are very useful for seeing the main outlines of a year: your holidays here, that major conference there, that key meeting or event in that period. But they are generally not easy to share because they give insufficient detail each day for action when people want to contact you. Some use a grid covering three months at a time, usually reproduced on an A4 sheet. This is easy for photocopying, but again does not contain enough space for detailed entries for each day.

The most useful system I know is a simple monthly sheet, as given on page 150. This has enough space to outline availability and key meetings and can be readily shared by photocopying it for senior colleagues, your spouse and any others who need it. The dates are put under each day, so that part of a month might look like this:

TUES 4	8.30 Mr Robinson 9.15 Mrs Stanfield 10.00 Mr Harrison 10.30—12 Prepare next year's budget 1.15—4.30 Architect re new buildings	TUES 11	9—11 Meet David in London 11.30—1 Travel back 2—4 Prepare talk for next Tuesday 4—5.30 Correspondence 7.45—10.30 Deacons	TUES 18	9—12 Free: reading time 12.30 Prayer meeting 2.15—4.15 Meet John at station for meeting 4.30—7 Prepare for weekend meeting 7.30 Alan and Mary for a meal	TUES 25	9—5 Training conference in London
WED 5	8.30 Plan next month's schedule 9.30—12 Team meeting 12—1.30 Team lunch 2—4.30 Write article 6+ Take wife out	WED 12	10 Monthly Communion 12 Lunch with Dick 2—5 Visiting in Station Road	WED 19	9.30—12 Team meeting 12—1.30 Team lunch 2—5 Meet elderly people at community centre 6—9 Council meeting	WED 26	(and so on)

It helps a great deal to include the length of each engagement. The purpose of this format is to identify your whereabouts and availability. Your spare time is implicit in the gaps.

Planning your diary

What kind of items are worth putting into your diary? What takes priority? I have found it helpful to mark in the following items as soon as I get my new diary:

'Leave blank' days. 'Leave blank' days are essentially days under your control, as far as that can be. They are days on

SUN	MON	TUE	WED	THU	FRI	SAT
SUN	MON	TUE	WED	THU	FRI	SAT
SUN	MON	TUE	WED	THU	FRI	SAT
SUN	MON	TUE	WED	THU	FRI	SAT
SUN	MON	TUE	WED	THU	FRI	SAT

which my secretary may not enter any meeting without my express permission. I try to have one such day a week, two the week before I go on holiday to help get the desk cleared and two the week I come back because the mail has mounted up.

These days are essentially 'buffer' days. They have the great advantage of allowing flexibility. If Thursday is my 'leave blank' day this week and someone phones on Tuesday asking to see me urgently, I can say, 'Can you come Thursday?' If they can only come on the Tuesday, can I move anything from the Tuesday to the Thursday to give them space to see me? 'Leave blank' days allow people access to you. If you are a leader, people will need to contact you sometimes at short notice. An accident occurs, someone is ill, perhaps someone dies, and you are involved. 'Leave blank' days give you freedom to give time without worrying that your programme is irretrievably affected.

How long should you keep 'leave blank' days before you release them for meetings? This depends on the nature of your work and the number of requests to see you at very short notice, but probably not more than a week before. Of course if nothing happens, no one wants to meet you, and the phone does not ring, you have a free day to work unhindered. Such days tend to be few and far between, but lovely to experience!

'Work at home' days. These are days which you set aside for planned work. If you work from home the title is inappropriate, but the principle is the same: time allocated specifically to doing something without interruption. This might be planning an event, analysing data, going through the notes you made on a course you attended, a time for extended prayer and meditation, preparation for a sermon or meeting you have to take, writing an article or chapter of a book, or anything else which needs your undivided attention. I try to make at least one day a fortnight a 'work at home' day. It may not be worked out actually at home—it may be in the office or elsewhere—but the purpose is to have a day when the phone does not interrupt you and you are able to think. Time to think is critical for leadership: here is a simple way to make it.

Days in lieu. In a survey of nearly a thousand clergy MARC Europe found that on average only 85 per cent take their days off, and of these 47 per cent are interrupted.[5] If you work extra hours because of the demands at work, or miss your day off, schedule in days in lieu. Perhaps you put two or three of them together to give you a long weekend or a mid-week break, but do not just let them go. Some organisations insist that any days in lieu must be taken by the end of the month after they were earned. The principle of taking them sometime is important, and if you need to plan that far ahead put them in your diary now. Make sure you take TOIL—Time Off In Lieu.

Team meetings. Getting away with your inner circle, key colleagues, other leaders is important. These occasions often provide the times when friendship and trust are built up, fellowship developed and you learn to enjoy your companions in an altogether new light. It frequently helps the process to meet for a day, or a weekend, away from home at a retreat centre, hotel, or other appropriate accommodation. It is important to have time to discuss issues of policy without the pressure of another engagement in an hour's time, or the need to get through the rest of your agenda. Here is the opportunity to plan creatively, to build vision, to think ahead, to pray together, to discuss in depth. A day a quarter is probably the minimum you need to generate effectiveness in your team. They need to be planned in advance so all can attend. These are not the normal daily or weekly operational meetings, but planned policy formulation meetings when it is essential to be able to listen to others, and to talk things through.

Reading days. These are essentially two or three 'work at home' days taken consecutively. Some take a week away from home every six months to read. You may be involved in a major project which needs very careful planning, and for which one day will not be enough. Writing, analysing, envisioning are often activities which need to span more than one day. Put such times in your diary now. A colleague suggested this some years ago, and I have found it a lifeline. These days are essential to help you keep up with all that is happening, but need to be planned into your diary the moment you get it. If effectiveness is one of your priorities, make reading days a priority in your planning!

Set a block calendar. The above categories deal with the macro, but what about the micro? Here is one idea to help ministers walk the tightrope between the two conflicting expectations of producing thoughtful sermons and being available to every church member when needed:[6]

- Divide waking hours into three four-hour blocks: 8—noon, 1—5 pm, 6—10 pm. This yields twenty-one blocks of time in a week, with space for meals and sleeping.
- Allocate twelve blocks (forty-eight hours) for church ministry.
- Accomplish priority items in that time.
- When a wedding or meeting falls on an 'off' block, swap it with a 'work' block.
- Recognise that a wedding or meeting normally takes a substantial portion of the day or evening. Work a full block of time.
- Schedule non-death emergencies into work blocks.

Controlling meetings

Shanahan's law says that the length of meeting is proportional to the square of the number of people present.[7] Another sceptic defined a meeting as 'an avenue into which good ideas are lured and quietly strangled'.[8] Few people work in isolation, and meetings to agree future actions and to co-ordinate progress are essential. How do you make meetings effective?

Over a thousand executives responded when asked what were the key components for an effective meeting.[9] They were (in order of importance):

- doing adequate preparation
- agreeing on follow-up actions
- having an effective chair
- staying on track
- setting clear objectives for the meeting.

Good preparation

They also found a strong correlation between preparation for meetings and subsequent productivity. In a 3M brochure the comment is made, 'In good meetings, heads nod in agreement. In bad meetings, heads merely nod.' How do we prepare for good meetings?

State purpose. Why is the meeting being held? What outcome is expected? Is it one of a series or a one-off? Is it regular or occasional? The meeting should expect to achieve results, by sharing information, solving problems, teaching or motivating people.

Give prior information. Give not only the starting time but the finishing time in advance also. State who is expected to attend. Help people to know the expected outcome by circulating papers sufficiently far in advance to allow them to be read and prayed over. Who is invited to come? The same 3M brochure asks, 'Are they the right people for solving the problem, making the decision, giving of their experience?' You need to have the right number of right people too: a major viewpoint is best expressed by more than one person, and preferably at least three.

Choose the right venue. The room you use sets the mood of the meeting. During an interregnum one Anglican church's Parochial Council met in someone's house. When the new minister arrived, the venue switched to the church hall and the hard uncomfortable seats associated with it. The 'atmosphere' of the meeting visibly changed. If only a few of you are meeting, do not use a ballroom!

State where the meeting will be held. Ensure also that adequate equipment is provided. Will any participant require an overhead projector? Is the screen big enough for all to see? Is a cassette player required? Is a jug of water and glasses to hand?

Start and finish on time. Even if nobody is present start the meeting on schedule. If you always wait till most people have come, and this takes fifteen minutes, you will always start a 7 pm meeting at 7.15 pm. Either change the time to 7.15 pm (but the actual start is then likely to drift to 7.30 pm), or (better by far) keep it at 7 pm, but start at the time stated. People will arrive punctually next time.

Likewise finish at the time indicated. If you have not finished the discussion say, 'We have only fifteen minutes left and we need longer to conclude this discussion. Can we agree to go on to 10.30 pm instead of 10.15 pm?' If the meeting agrees fine; if not, curtail the discussion and put it on the agenda for the next meeting, or, if too urgent for that, suggest an extra meeting to resolve the issue. But keep to your stipulated length.

Effective agendas

The agenda is critical for a good meeting. It is often worth indicating on it how long you intend to discuss each item. This enables the chair to say, 'We have just ten more minutes on this item. Who else would like to comment? Well, if you are brief, we have time for both of you, and then we'll decide on the resolution and move on to the next item.' This enforces movement, keeping to the priorities implicit in the timing of items, and curtails unnecessary discussion.

Most agendas contain different types of items. These are:

Standing items. These include items such as apologies of absence, minutes of the last meeting, matters arising not covered in main agenda, reports of progress on projects, financial reports, descriptions of places visited, conferences attended or people met, and like items. *If a meeting consists only of standing items, cancel it:* such information can invariably be circulated or hold over to the next meeting. Meeting simply to get information is a waste of time when other efficient communication mechanisms exist.

Decision items. These are the items on which a decision is to be made at that meeting. They may well be supported by a paper with the draft resolution for approval stated. But tell attenders before the meeting that these are the crucial issues to be resolved on this occasion.

Discussion items. These are items at which no decision will be taken at the forthcoming meeting, although they may require decision subsequently. They are the key items of interest for volunteers serving on a committee. If you have professional people sitting on your deacons panel or Parochial Church Council, say, they will feel really able to help when allowed to express their views on such issues. Their rapport will be built up when involved in formulating policy, especially if it relates to their speciality. It is always worth having at least one such item on the agenda, but not more than three.

With each of these items, know who will be the presenter or leader in giving the information or leading the discussion. It is helpful to put his or her name after the appropriate item. So a typical agenda might look like this (the items in square brackets give explanation and would not normally be included):

AGENDA
for Meeting of the Deacons on Wednesday 12th July
at the Church Hall from 7.30 to 10 pm

7.30 **1** Opening prayer (John to lead)   [John is not the pastor]

7.40 **2** Information Items

       2a Apologies for absence (Mary)   [Mary is secretary]

       2b Minutes of previous meeting (Philip)
                          [Philip is chairman]

       2c Matters arising not included below (All)
                          [Anyone may lead]

       2d Meeting with local churches (Norman)
                          [Norman is pastor]

       2e Progress on plans for visiting each week (Norman)

       2f Financial report (Yvonne)   [Yvonne is treasurer]

       2g Visit of superintendent in November (Norman)

8.10 **3** Decision Items

  8.10   3a Finalisation of training programme next year (Philip)
                        (Paper already circulated)

  8.30   3b Redecoration of church (Joan)
                   [Joan heads up the working party]
          (Agreement to tenders on work and programme previously agreed; please bring previous papers, and see tenders attached.)

8.55 **4** Break for coffee

9.10 **5** Discussion Items

  9.10   5a Do we need a church administrator? Preliminary considerations. (Norman and All) (See paper attached).

  9.45   5b Change of date of next meeting (Philip)

       5c Confirmation of deacons' Away Days next year (Philip)

  9.50   5d Any other business (Philip)

10.00 **6** Closing prayer (June)   [June is a deacon]

Seven different people are named as being specifically involved in the meeting. The chairman and pastor naturally appear most frequently. They do not have to be the same person. Very often the meeting can proceed much more smoothly if someone other than the minister chairs it. Similarly in an office situation the senior person present does not have to chair every meeting—delegating that responsibility can often save time and release (and develop) latent skills in others. Delegation of chairing can leave you freer to express your views unhindered by having also to control the discussion. Note coffee comes in the middle of the meeting, not the beginning. Two other agenda items need comment.

Any other business (AOB). This can be a pitfall for the unwary. It is useful for the chair to identify at the start of the meeting any AOB items members have and thus judge how long to leave for them. He or she can also rule that an item is too major for brief consideration at the tail end of the meeting, and suggest putting it on the agenda next time for full consideration.

Ruling that all AOB items must be cleared through the chair before the start of the meeting tends to be inhibiting and is undemocratic. Some suggest that AOB items will be allowed only if they relate to matters which have arisen since the agenda was circulated. It does not matter how AOB is dealt with, so long as surprises are saved—there is nothing better designed to kill the feeling of a meeting than a minor item being raised and discussed at long length when everyone is dying to get home!

Review the meeting. Occasionally, perhaps once a year, include under the discussion items such as 'Review of this meeting'. Discuss how long it should be, where it should be held, its frequency. Was the meeting well or badly run? How much real progress was made? Was the group cohesive, or did it tend to fragment and polarise? Did most of the members contribute or was the time dominated by a small number? Were the goals of the meeting clear? Did you stick to the goals and agenda or wander? Could the meeting have been shortened? If so, how? What one change would you make for next time the group meets?[10] This gives the opportunity to consider how business is conducted outside the framework of how a particular item is handled, and invariably leads to fruitful ideas on how meetings can be improved—the break for coffee mid-meeting, as in the above example, came directly out of a discussion in a review of a meeting.

Effective chairing

Much of the quality of a meeting depends on how it is chaired. After one meeting when the usual chairman was absent, one member wrote to him, 'We need you! Murray.' Such notes always encourage. Here are eight rules for good committee chairing, based in part on a former Secretary to the Cabinet's advice:[11]

Know the key issues. Good chairs prepare thoroughly and can speak, if necessary, on any item on the agenda. They will know the objectives of the meeting and work towards them throughout. As they ought to keep their eyes on the speaker, they cannot shuffle notes or turn back to odd paragraphs for reminders, and so on.[12] Homework not only is essential, but should include any necessary discussions in advance on points of difficulty.

Know the desired outcome. Not every decision is along the lines suggested. But those in the chair need to know what the desired result is and why. They need to be sure all sides of the argument are presented fairly by allowing more than one person to speak where necessary. They should remind members of the decision required, should not reveal their personal view too early, and if they want to make a major contribution, need to separate that from the role of chairing.

Know the dynamics of the participants. This is not always possible or easy to do in advance. With regular meetings obviously everyone gets to know each other over time. One important difference, however, is the role of the two sexes in meetings. A Harvard University study of children's games showed that boys' games have longer and more rules, and that boys enjoyed fighting over the rules as much as the game. Girls, however, tended to suspend the game if the rules got in the way. To them relationships were more important than rules.[13] The same is true in meetings. Men by and large assume that if people want to speak, they will take the initiative to do so. Women often assume that at some point they will be asked for their input. Women need to be encouraged to contribute and men to invite women into the conversation.[14] Women used to dislike interrupting men, but this is changing with the advent of much assertiveness training. Likewise cross-cultural differences must be taken into consideration if those from the Two-Thirds world are present. A good chairperson is sensitive to these differences.

Prepare your opening. Do this for the opening of the meeting and for each item which the chair introduces. Those in the chair should be factual, cheerful, topical, and need to remember their goals. They need to capture their audience each time to prepare them for active involvement in that item, or introduce them appropriately to the speaker. If the subject matter is complicated, it is worth saying how the discussion will be handled (for example, splitting up the matter into component parts, or elucidating factual points first, or letting everyone give a general viewpoint, or going through the paper paragraph by paragraph).

Keep to time. The chair should assure the meeting that this will be done. If the meeting gets behind schedule the chair should mention it and take a decision to extend the meeting, or delay certain items, well ahead of the end when lack of time makes discussion hurried and decisions inadequately considered. The speaker for each topic should be briefed in advance where necessary.

Give clear and fair summaries. When chairing you must be neutral in your summing up of discussion and ensure that any further actions are precisely formulated. You must therefore be alert, and listen without interrupting. Focus on the issues, not personalities. State quite shortly what you understand to be the main points of a long intervention. If necessary take a vote, though often the mind of the meeting will emerge in the discussion. If a vote is close be very cautious about proceeding. Usually it is better to rediscuss the issue so that a consensus, or as great a consensus as possible, can emerge. State the final position clearly if more time is needed to reach a conclusion.

But try to come to a decision if you can; look for signs that someone with a minority view is willing to change his/her mind, and help let him/her off the hook.

Stay courteous and in control. Ultimately the chair has to involve other members (or dissuade them from involvement if they are too active), but must not allow his or her position to be usurped, nor be rude to the offending party. Be brisk and firm with red herrings and trivia and do not allow old ground to be covered unless new information is likely to emerge which will really make a difference. Take the heat out of difficult situations by light-hearted comment, or the introduction of a new contributor.[15]

End positively. Thank people for coming, especially if the meeting has been long or tedious. Congratulate someone on his/her promotion, fiftieth birthday, new grandchild, or whatever. Be involved so that there is something nice to end with, something to thank God for specially.

Minutes should be crisp, clean, and contain records of decisions made, not the discussion that led to them.

Effective control

It is easy to write that the chair should stay in control. Sometimes that is easier said than done! It may be necessary for you to handle the following types of participants:[16]

Hecklers, the ones who want to shout down the chair. If the leader responds in kind, an intellectual duel follows. It is better to use peer pressure by inviting the rest of the group to judge the criticisms being made, which usually results in the group affirming the leader's position. If a heckler continues, institutionalise the criticism by indicating how useful it is to have so many points of disagreement identified, and ask the heckler to be official devil's advocate—to make a special effort to indicate every point in which the group is going astray. He will thus be seen as making a positive contribution to the argument, usually the reverse of his intentions.

Know-alls, who keep interrupting with explanations or supplying unnecessary further details. Ask them to present a point, or tie them up in some positive task such as acting as ombudsman 'to keep the group up to speed'. The know-all thus acts in the limelight positively, the role usually desired.

Whisperers, who start side conversations during a meeting. A good chair will politely stop talking, wait till the whispers subside, and then continue. If the whispering persists the chair should welcome all contributions to the debate, and encourage all passing thoughts to be aired. Whisperers, under the piercing stare of many eyes, usually then either cease to talk or address their comments to the chair.

Silent ones, the quiet and timid participants. Encouragement by asking a simple direct question and praising the sagacity of the answer may be too transparent. Make sure you know who they are, and then, with eyes on the talkative ones, point out that some shy and quiet participants get a great deal from the meetings and do not need to contribute verbally. You are thereby slowly encouraging them to speak and not to feel labelled as shy and quiet.

Hair-splitters are characterised by great intolerance of generalities, ambiguity and analogy. They see themselves as the guardians of wisdom and logic. Hair-splitters disrupt because they focus on detail, which hinders consensus on the whole. The person in the chair needs to welcome all attempts to preserve accuracy, explain that some points are simplified for purposes of discussion, and ask the hair-splitter to make a written list of his points. Subsequently the chair will agree with these points and privately ask the hair-splitter how the generality is best presented, add to the points covered any which the hair-splitter had not noticed and then ask the hair-splitter to read both his points and suggestions at the next discussion.

Doodlers enormously irritate some, but are of no consequence to others. Try not to be annoyed with doodlers. If others get fascinated by the doodling, however, choose an appropriate moment, and indicate how much you like the doodles. Could the doodler serve the whole group by making a concise drawing or cartoon of each major agenda item? If so, supply him or her with transparencies and overhead projector pens.

Handling interruptions

The phone rang for the sixth time that hour. Someone knocked on the door. There were two urgent items in the mail that morning. How was next Sunday's sermon, or talk, going to be prepared? This was your first and only spare morning this week. Such situations are all too frequent. How do we cope with interruptions?

Fig 15: 'So I thought you could pick up the children'

Limit your availability

This is the heart of the matter. But how dare a pastor, called to serve the church and the members associated with it, do that? How can an executive caught up in a fulfilling job, with a major project to hand, not listen to others? In the film *Time to Think*, Peter Reynolds, a harassed manager, said that in as many words to his boss, who told him what to do, and then said, 'Just do it.'

It is, after all, what Jesus did. He sent His disciples out one day without Him. He gave them instructons on what to take, where to go ('the house of Israel'), what to do ('heal the sick'), how to react if no one wanted their peace. He did not go with them—He limited His availability. They had to cope with the problems of the mission somehow themselves.

On another occasion He did not immediately go up to the Passover celebration at the Temple. The disciples had to answer as best they could questions such as, 'Is He coming?' 'Where will He be?' Jesus was not there.

When the Jews wanted to make Him king after the feeding of the five thousand, Jesus spent the night alone on the mountain to pray. He was not with the disciples on the lake. They were by themselves.

Sometimes Jesus healed all who came to Him, but at the pool of Bethesda He healed just one man who had been there for thirty-eight years. Why not the others? Did they not need His healing touch also? Doubtless, but He limited himself to this one man. At Jacob's well, Jesus spoke to the woman present. Why did He not come back later and speak to all the other women getting water? He was simply not available. Jesus was neither constantly available nor equally available.[17]

Perhaps the reason in part was to help the disciples grow through delegation; we are bidden to present each person maturing in Christ Jesus. Sometimes, as on the mountain, He wanted privacy. At the well, He desired refreshment. At other times, He needed rest. His purpose was to bring the flock to fullness and dependence on God. Of course, Christ knew the Holy Spirit would come, but the desire was to help the disciples to cope when He was physically not there. We likewise have to help our people cope when the leader is not physically present, and we do that in part simply by not being available.

If you follow through the suggestions made earlier concerning the organisation of your diary, there will be times when you are not available to others. You are not saying that your members may not see you, but that they may not see you now. Your job is to lead, to pastor, to encourage, to envision, not to be constantly available at every one's beck and call. In this you are simply following the Master.

Jesus said 'No' to the crowd who would make Him king. He said 'No' to Peter's suggestion concerning the cross. He said 'I am He' to the woman at the well, but not to the Pharisees who asked for a sign to show He was the Messiah. We sometimes likewise must say 'No' to people's suggestions, either collectively or individually. That may be a fine principle, but how do we do it in practice?

Your work is serious

We have to earn the right to work without interruption.[18] We have to tell others that our work is serious, and the time we have to spend on it is an investment for them. So let people know you value your time. Put up a big clock that both you and your visitors can see.

'I'm sorry, John, I can't talk to you now. I'm preparing my sermon. Could I phone you back this afternoon?' What does such a message do? Communicate to John that preparing your sermon is real work, that time is precious (especially mornings when many people are at their freshest). You also tell him, however, that you are concerned and that you will gladly listen to him at a more convenient occasion. If John wants to ask you something urgently ('But my mother is dying. Can you come to the hospital?'), he will still tell you and you can then decide whether visiting John's mother is now more important than preparing your sermon. Such adrenalin producers may not happen often, but they are non-negotiable.[19] But if John merely wanted to talk over his concerns about, say, the young people's work, this can properly wait till later.

You have to discern his real reason for contacting you, which is not always the initial topic. So ask, therefore, the purpose of the call: 'What is the topic we need to discuss?' Such a filtering procedure is a fairly standard secretarial routine.

Minimise interruption time

Keep interruptions short, when they are allowed. Work out who really needs access to you and delegate other interruptions. Be ruthless with time, gracious with people. Postpone the non-urgent demands and reschedule them to suit your convenience.

'I'm up against a deadline now. Could we discuss it at coffee break?'

'I'm in a meeting now. Could you please phone Stephen to sort that out?'

'I'd love to ask you in, Anne, but I'm working now on the plans for a special project for next week. Would you mind if we met on Thursday week instead?'

'I'm right in the middle of a report now. This sounds like something you can handle, but if you really get stuck, come back to me after lunch.'

'I'm working on a presentation for Wednesday. Why not jot down your thoughts and bring the matter up at the staff meeting next week?'

'I'd like to hear more about that but I can't spare the time now. Let's have lunch together on Friday.'

Positively this means that you need to let people know what you do. Many parishioners have little idea what their vicar does during the week. Tell them! Keep your PCC or your deacons or elders well informed. Ask them to pray about certain parts of your schedule. Let that schedule include 'leave blank' days when people know you are available. Such visibility then aids invisibility at other times. As far as you can, anticipate people's demands on you and work to meet these in advance if possible.[20]

A mnemonic for different ways of dealing with people making demands on you is GRACES, and sometimes we need them![21] It stands for:

G	Greet	A quick 'hello' and then continue with your work. Anything more might open the floodgates.
R	Receive	A couple of sentences rather than just one word, while definitely retaining control.
A	Accompany	Escorting them to someone who can deal with their problem, usually your secretary or subordinate at work. Then immediately return to your work.
C	Confer	This is often a 'people' situation that you judge requires your immediate time, but keep it relatively short. Allow ten minutes.

| E | Embrace | This is for something both serious and urgent. A cuppa is called for! It may well distract you from other plans. |
| S | See off | Far more polite than 'shut up!' and also more effective. You cannot see them now but would be delighted to do so at an alternative time. |

Practise prevention

One minister I know went each morning to work in his vestry, where there was no phone. Another works in his garden caravan. Someone once humorously asked if Jesus would still go into the desert today. The answer was 'Yes, because there is no telephone there!' The telephone can be a menace. It is legitimate, however, to dial your own number and after a minute or so the engaged tone stops. People then cannot reach you. A former employee of MARC Europe used to unplug her telephone half an hour before supper so that she and her husband could have their meal in peace. (It was plugged in again only after the washing up was done!) Others have answerphones which allow people access to you by leaving a message which you can follow through at your own convenience.

Some people in an office situation work with their door open if they do not mind visitors, and with the door shut when they have a meeting or are concentrating on some item. Such a system gives an unambiguous message.

Others arrange their environment to discourage casual visitors. In one open plan office where I worked a colleague moved his desk into a corner, put a cupboard in front of him, a screen by the side, a further screen to the side of that, then a filing cabinet. It was like solving Hampton Court maze to find him, but he was able to concentrate on his work.

Arrange interception

This is not always possible but if you have a secretary ensure all telephone calls and visitors go through her. Some men working from home are fortunate in that their wives will act similarly.

It is also possible to arrange to be interrupted after so many minutes of the meeting have passed. One senior colleague allowed people to see him for only thirty minutes at a time. I wanted to know what happened if you overstayed your welcome and kept on talking beyond the half hour. Sure enough, after thirty-two minutes, his secretry came in with a (rather well worn) piece of card which stated, 'Your next visitor is here.' He immediately stood up, said, 'Nice meeting you, Mr Brierley. Look forward to seeing you again,' and went to welcome his new visitor.

Standing up is always useful, and not only when you have a bad back. It communicates that you want a short meeting. Or perch on the edge of the desk. Where possible meet other than at your office—it is always easier to leave than to throw someone out.

Limit self-made interruptions

Not all interruptions are external. You can easily make some yourself. For example, you may have several telephone calls to make. Making them sporadically interrupts the flow of what you are doing. So plan to make your important calls all at one time. You will spend less time on arranging to phone and the actual call in this way.

If you find you have several things to tell someone else, such as your secretary, do not call her every time something comes up. Make a note so that you can tell her everything at once. That saves her time and yours.

If you are in the middle of a job and your biro runs out go and get a refill but do not decide to restock all your stationery. That constitutes an unnecessary time interrupter.

Some interruptions, of course, are inevitable. We may work all day skipping lunch. We might be able to work all night as well, but this can often be a false economy with time, because skipped meals leads to flagging energy, with consequential loss of concentration. Eventually we have to eat and sleep. When that happens be grateful for what you have accomplished, not fretful over what you have not done.

Using the telephone

The telephone has become a fact of modern life. Of all the households in Great Britain, 39 per cent had a phone in 1970, 72 per cent in 1980, and 87 per cent in 1989.[22] But the fact that it is commonplace does not mean that all know how to use it to the greatest advantage. The following notes, taken from the MARC Europe seminar on telephone usage, cover basic techniques.[23]

The telephone operator in an organisation or church reflects the image of that body. A quiet helpful voice suggests warmth and efficiency, a long wait or a gruff tone suggests the operator is doing you a favour by answering the call! It is important, therefore, that the person who answers the phone is trained to a high degree of proficiency, whether that person is the receptionist or the individual at the desk.

General points of technique

Do not keep people 'hanging on'. Let them know what is happening. If you cannot get an extension answered because it is engaged, say so. If you have to look something up, explain that you will be only a few moments; if it is likely to take longer arrange to phone back.

Use your telephone properly. Read the operating instructions for your telephone system, and make full use of its capabilities. Save time, for example, by using redial buttons, or the facility which allows a number to be dialled with the receiver still on so that you can work on until the call is actually answered. When you use the telephone hold it properly. There is no need to shout or whisper, unless you have a portable or car telephone when speaking especially clearly helps.

Be courteous. Not only say please and thank you, but be pleasant and smile as you would in face-to-face conversation. Vary your tone and the pace of your speech. Do not slouch when you use the telephone as you can easily get out of breath. Do not eat, chew, drink, cough, smoke, sniff or sneeze when using the telephone—and if a sneeze does come suddenly give warning and apologise afterwards! If you have to talk to someone else in the office, cover the mouthpiece, but remember the caller may still be able to hear you. If you have a phone you can use without holding the hand receiver, do remember that your voice sounds as if you are in a dustbin, or deep chasm. Always explain when you are not using your handset.

Be efficient. If you promise to phone someone, keep the promise even if there is nothing to report. If you let someone down, phone first rather than waiting for that person to complain. Be firm, not aggressive, expressing yourself simply, not speaking too quickly or using unexplained anger. If you need an order number, or other identification information, ask for it. Confirm a request in writing if necessary. If a call comes through to you by mistake, give the caller the name of the correct person and transfer him/her; if this is not possible, arrange for that person to phone the caller back. If you are going to be away from your desk, arrange for someone else to take your calls, or use an answerphone if you have one.

Incoming calls

Be efficient here too. Always answer the telephone promptly. A maximum of three rings should be the target. Keep a note pad and pen beside the telephone; special preprinted pads headed 'Telephone message' are available. Calls from portable or car phones often get cut off because reception is hindered as the vehicle goes under a bridge. There is often more crackle on the line. If the phone goes dead, keep saying 'Hello, can you hear me?' since often the reception works well one way and only intermittently the other.

Be courteous here also. Always greet the caller 'Good morning/afternoon', and introduce yourself ('Accounts department—John Smith speaking'). Some using a phone at home prefer to give their number. Offer service: 'How can I help you?'. Get the caller's name, and if you cannot catch it ask him/her to spell it. If you are unable to handle the query, take the caller's number so that someone else can phone back easily.

Listen attentively. Let the caller know you are listening by saying, 'Yes', 'Right', 'Fine'. If you do not understand, ask for clarification, and make notes to avoid forgetting. If necessary ask the caller to repeat the comments, and say you are writing them down. Summarise action points at the end of the call, and then try to deal with the matter immediately. Always thank people for calling.

Be directive. Sometimes the person at the other end of the phone is too talkative. Try to get the conversation back on track with phrases such as 'So you called about...' or 'I've got an appointment in a few minutes and I'm going to have to run', or 'I'm expecting another call about now; could we agree to do so and so?'

Outgoing calls

Know your numbers. Do not guess a number, always check it. Keeping a list of personal numbers is very useful, and their extensions, if appropriate. If a call is cut off, the original caller should redial.

Plan your calls. When you phone know what you want to phone about, have the relevant paperwork to hand. After the call note down what you decided and the date. Keep these reminders for as long as necessary, perhaps as a permanent part of your files. If a memo or letter is required, write or dictate it immediately while the call is still fresh in your mind. Save your small talk for the pub or fellowship meetings. It is cheaper to phone after 1 pm. Be aware of time passing on the phone.

Introduce yourself. Do not assume you are necessarily talking to the right person just because the telephone has been answered. Allow the person answering time to introduce herself, or ask, 'May I speak to Betty Hardcastle please?' Introduce yourself too, and give the name of your organisation or church, where relevant. Indicate why you are phoning, and keep to the point. If the other digresses bring him/her back to the subject—he/she is wasting your money and your time!

Dial your own calls. Someone else dialling for you does not save you much time and may give the impression that you think your time is more precious than the person you are contacting.

Likes and dislikes

What do people most appreciate when using the phone and find most annoying? A group were asked these questions and gave the following answers, with obvious implications for all telephone users:

POSITIVE FEATURES	NEGATIVE FEATURES
Quick answer to the dialling tone.	Abrupt response and a sense of 'couldn't care less'.
Politeness, helpfulness and friendly voice.	Being passed from extension to extension.
A sufficient knowledge of their own organisation to direct you properly.	The other party not calling back when he or she promised to do so.
Clear speech and a listening ear.	The other party putting the phone down and cutting you off.
Information on what is happening.	Keeping you waiting if the person is unattainable.
Courtesy with names and information.	Having to repeat information (such as your name and organisation) several times to different people.

Overcoming procrastination

There are times when we all feel less like working than we should. A snowstorm in the middle of mock 'A' level exams made my youngest son choose sledging rather than revising. A TV programme catches our eye and we watch instead of work. We get up tired from a late night and moan rather than move.

Procrastination is being dilatory, deferring action. How do we help ourselves to take action and start again trying to make effective use of our time? We may need to stop socialising, day dreaming or dealing with peripheral items. Old procrastinators never die; they just keep putting it off![24]

Are you a procrastinator? Rate yourself on the following quiz.[25]

	Strongly Agree	Slightly Agree	Slightly Disagree	Strongly Disagree
I invent reasons and look for excuses for not acting on a tough problem.	☐	☐	☐	☐
It takes pressure for me to get on with a difficult assignment.	☐	☐	☐	☐
I take half measures which will avoid or delay unpleasant or difficult action.	☐	☐	☐	☐
There are too many interruptions and crises that interfere with my accomplishing the big jobs.	☐	☐	☐	☐
I avoid forthright answers when pressed for an unpleasant decision.	☐	☐	☐	☐
I have been guilty of neglecting follow-up aspects of important plans.	☐	☐	☐	☐
I try to get other people to do the unpleasant tasks for me.	☐	☐	☐	☐
I schedule big jobs late in the day, or take them home to do in the evening or weekends.	☐	☐	☐	☐
I've been too tired, nervous, or upset to do the difficult jobs that face me.	☐	☐	☐	☐
I like to get everything cleared off my desk before commencing a tough job.	☐	☐	☐	☐

Now score 4 points for every tick in the 'strongly agree' column, 3 points for every tick in the next column, 2 for each in the next, and 1 for each in the 'strongly disagree' column.

If your total score is 20 or under you are not a procrastinator but might occasionally have a problem. If you score 21—30 you have a procrastination problem, but not too severe. If you score over 30 you probably have frequent and severe problems of procrastinating. So read on!

Recall your vision

What do you want to be remembered for? What will the pastor say about you at your funeral? What do you want to do with your life? The anonymous fourteenth-century author of *The Cloud of Unknowing* includes these lines: 'It is neither what you are nor what you have been that God sees with his all merciful eyes, but what you desire to be.' If you are feeling off colour, recall what you wish to be. Spend time in prayer. 'You are what you pray.' Rise with a fresh determination to conquer the world, as it were. To wish is fruitless unless you act, however little. (You cannot learn German in a weekend, but you can order a book or cassette from the library on Saturday.)

Do some planning

Plan the tasks you have to do, especially if you are engaged in a large project. Subdivide the work into smaller components. Be realistic! Organise people who must be involved and the information required. Delegate parts of it. Schedule it into a sensible time frame. Protect the blocks of time allocated for it and, if you can, do the tough bits when your energy level is high. You may not be able to prepare all your sermon today, but can you complete the first point? Punch holes in the over-whelming task, and reduce it to bite-size pieces.[26]

A woman wanted to decorate her living room but found it difficult because her children needed her attention. So she allocated fifteen minutes per day—time to peel off one strip of wallpaper. The following week she washed the walls, the week after, the floor. Eventually, after five weeks, the job was done.

Planning involves identifying priorities. What must be done, should be done, would be done? When you have done that, stick to them—that is what prioritisation is all about. If you have an unpleasant letter to write, an awkward person to see, an apology to make, a difficult visit, do that first. Writing or dictating the hard letter first frees you to write the next six easily. If you write the easier six first your mind continues to jump to the hard one and you do not concentrate properly. So you save time as well as find release by tackling the worst job first.

Do not fritter your time away with self-imposed time wasters. Your pencils do not need sharpening again—you did them all yesterday. Those sheets do have to be stapled together, but do it when you are tired, not fresh. Be productive, not just busy. Spend the first five minutes of each day planning with your secretary or someone else.

Identify why you are procrastinating

Sometimes ask yourself not what you have to do but what is not being done, and why. Some years ago I took up part of our patio and then left it for months. The patio included a drain cover and relaying it meant raising this half an inch, something I did not know how to do without breaking it. The patio was not relaid because I lacked the time, energy or money, but the technical knowledge of how to cope with a drain cover.

What is it that you are not doing? What is not being done in your church? What is your organisation not achieving? Why not? Discuss the question with your team, your elders, deacons, or PCC. It can often lead to fruitful ways of thinking round the problem.

What is the price of delay? What do you lose by not taking action now? Are you really running away from the job because it is too difficult or complicated? What happens if this job is not done now? Not done ever? Have you still got the previous task unfinished? If so, complete that first. What excuses are you making for failing to start?[27]

Get yourself going

Make a commitment to someone else. Tell your spouse or church secretary what you will do today or this week. The involvement of a second person, like a witness to a promise, can act as a goad to action. It is harder to make excuses to another person for not getting the job done.

Arrange or rearrange your environment. If your desk faces the window and you are distracted, turn your desk around. You aren't paid to count the raindrops! In one of his seminars on relieving stress, Baptist minister Rowland Croucher advises you to work in one direction in your study, to pray looking in another direction (perhaps over a garden) and to counsel in a third direction; such change releases greater concentration. Put distractions like the television, the magazine rack, or whatever beckons, irresistibly out of the way.

Give yourself rewards along the way. When we were choosing the title of a quarterly bulletin we took an hour considering all the alternatives, and then someone said, 'Let's have a cup of coffee while we're talking.' 'No, we'll get the title first and then we'll break for coffee'—and we agreed the title in five minutes flat! Promise yourself a chocolate once you have finished that letter. Promise yourself you will work till eleven tonight and then sleep later tomorrow. When you have lost two stone you will go and buy yourself a new suit.

Turn the tasks into a game. You have done twenty of these in the past hour, can you do twenty-two in the next hour? A huge mailing was being organised and the letters had to go out urgently. So we did the job together with taped music in the background. Having fun in your work can often help the wheels to go round.

Stress the benefits. 'Once we've rebuilt the foundations,' Nehemiah might have said, 'the actual walls around Jerusalem will not be so difficult. As the walls get higher so it will be harder for the enemy to rush us in surprise. With the gate towers almost built we can start refitting the huge gates, which will give us much greater security.' Thinking positively of the consequences of each action can help motivation.

Be positive

John Haggai writes in his book *Lead On!*:[28]

> After telling of his misery and misfortune Job said, 'For the thing I greatly feared had come upon me, and what I dreaded has happened to me.'[29] Job feared the worst and he got it.

Our negative thoughts and fears become self-fulfilling prophecies. If you don't believe you will make your sales goal, you probably won't. If you are a pastor and you are afraid your new congregation won't accept you, they probably won't. If you tell a child that he will fail and never amount to any good, you'll probably be right. So many dear people see the glass half empty instead of half full. They don't comprehend that 'God has not given us a spirit of fear, but of power and of love and of a sound mind.'[30]

You'll ruin your leadership potential by concentrating on the things you don't want. But if you keep your mind on the things you want, you'll probably succeed. Keeping your mind on winning the race is the first step to making it a reality. Believing a friend can accomplish a difficult task and telling him he can do it can help to make it possible.

When Winston Churchill spoke to the nation on 18th June 1940, the day after France fell to Germany, he concluded positively: 'Let us therefore brace ourselves to our duties, and so bear ourselves that if the British Empire and its Commonwealth last for a thousand years, men will still say: *This* was their finest hour!'

Retrieving material noted in talks

When you are studying formally you constantly take notes of lectures. This habit should continue as you attend conferences, hear talks, listen to sermons, read books, scan articles, or gather information in any other way. How can you organise this, so that, like a good filing system, you can find what you have noted?

Key principles

The following suggestions relate to a more personal system than the office or church system described previously. Your purpose is to save time when you want to refer back to some input you previously had.

Keep papers together. Be systematic as to how you keep your notes. This may be in a loose-leaf binder, which may be added to as necessary, and has the advantage that odd sheets, say torn from a magazine, can be holed and put in the appropriate place. Or you may use files in a filing cabinet, or wallets kept together. These both have the advantage of clear external marking and can take any size paper you may wish to add, but the papers are not then so easily kept in order.

Mark papers consistently. Put the subject clearly at the top, say the right-hand side for the front of a piece of paper and left-hand side for the back so that the numbers are always on the outward side. Use numerical codes or a simple alphabetical abbreviation—the latter is easier to remember—such as: ECH (Early Church History); ST (Systematic Theology). Three letters should be sufficient. Then number every page, that is, both sides of each leaf.

If you subsequently want to add extra pages label them appropriately, for example, ECH2a and ECH2b between pages ECH2 and ECH3. If you add a magazine article note the magazine's name if it does not appear, and the month and year of issue: you may want to quote it later and give details of its source. Noting it now saves time chasing it later.

The categories can be kept in any convenient or logical order, but if other than alphabetical it may be helpful to have an alphabetical list so you know what categories you already have, and, if kept in more than one place, where each may be found.

Index systematically. A loose-leaf book with twenty-six pages labelled A—Z can form a simple index. Note names of individuals, new headings, events, by the major word. Use surnames for individuals: 'Luther, Martin' thus comes under L. 'Anastasis' might be either under 'anastasis' if you can remember the Greek, or under the translation 'resurrection', but whichever you use be consistent: do not index some under the original language and some under the translation. Index under the key word: for example, 'Council of Trent' under 'Trent, Council of', not under C. But do not worry if all the entires under H, say, are not in alphabetical order. Your eye can scan quite

quickly down non-alphabetical entries given the initial letter.
Thus a section might look like:

> Hus, John
> Hell, gates of
> Holiness of God
> Hunter, A.M.
> Herod the Great
> Humanism
> Hebrews, Book of
> Hasmoneans
> Hades—see Hell

If your entries are short, you can get more on a page by
having more than one column. If, for a popular subject, you use
up all the space, do not cram more in underneath—it is difficult
to read and you may still not have enough room. Simply put an
arrow at the end of the line to indicate a further entry later,
which will have the same title followed by '(cont'd)' to show
there is a previous entry.

Index Scripture. Put any Scripture references in the left margin
of notes you take so that later you can write in the text or the
relevant part of it on the same line. This aids subsequent reference a great deal, eases revision for examinations, reinforces
the argument, and can save much time later in looking up
passages. So, for example, under the heading 'Who was Mark?'
in a lecture on that Gospel:

Acts 12:12	Mary, the mother of John whose other name was Mark.
12:25	Barnabas and Saul returned from Jerusalem...bringing...John.
13:5	at Salamis...they had John to assist them.
13:13	Paul...set sail...John left them and returned to Jerusalem.
15:37	Barnabas wanted to take John called Mark.
15:39	Barnabas took Mark with him and sailed away to Cyprus.
Col 4:10	Mark the cousin of Barnabas.

2 Tim 4:11   Get Mark and bring him with you for he is very useful in serving me.

Philem 24   sends greetings to you and so do Mark...and Luke my fellow workers.

1 Pet 5:13   ...sends you greetings; and so does my son Mark.

Have a separate index for each book of the Bible, and index the appropriate passages either as 1:6, meaning chapter 1 verse 6, or 2:8–10, meaning verses 8 to 10 of chapter 2. So a section from Daniel might look like:

3:17	D3	[D = Daniel]
9:24	ST411	[ST = Systematic Theology]
2:44	NT43, ST657	
		[NT = New Testament Introduction]
9:24–27	ST438,504, D14,35, ST702,716	
10:12,13	GC26a, D48	[GC = Gospels Content]

Begin now. The longer you leave it the more material is excluded from your classification and index. Note the date you start, so that everything from that date onwards is indexed. If you want to index earlier material go back systematically. Lest the scheme seems overwhelming, reckon on going backwards only as and when you have time to do a thorough job. Your start date becomes more important with time, and your earlier material perhaps less necessary to index fully.

This kind of system is adaptable to material other than notes and loose papers. Books can be put into such a system (index by abbreviating the title using its initial letters, so *Priorities, Planning and Paperwork* becomes simply PPP). A list of these abbreviations and where you keep the book is essential for subsequent location. If you lend a book you can note this alongside your entry so you do not go hunting for it thinking you have misplaced it.

I use a similar system for my overhead projector slides and note when I use which for a particular talk, so that I can either repeat the sequence or avoid those slides if speaking to the same group again.

The fundamental purpose is always to save time. Retrieval and access to material is frequently needed by ministers and others, and in the fight for time this type of system, which can be adapted as required to the needs of each individual, aids that fight. Save future hours by spending a few minutes now in ensuring easy access to your material.

Your system is after all 'a reflection of personal style. Transferable? You be the judge. But what is important is that any system be simple, quickly usable, reflective of your thinking and style, and up-to-date. Beyond that, all it needs is regular attention.'[31]

Delegation

In the fight for time, giving tasks to other people can be crucial. It not only helps save your time, but changes a one-person activity into a working organisation,[32] whether they be full-time employees or volunteers. In the earlier chapter on priorities, delegating was identified as relevant when you are faced with an important piece of work that is not urgent. As noted in Chapter 2, there are, though, three things that you may never delegate to others: your vision, your involvement with your family, and your care of yourself.

Why are Christian leaders so reluctant to delegate? Dr Ted Engstron gives five reasons.[33] They:

- believe that those asked will not be able to do the job
- fear competition from others
- are afraid of losing recognition
- think their own weakness will be exposed
- feel they will not have the time to check the work and give proper training.

At a MARC Europe seminar, Christian leaders were asked why they should delegate, and gave the following reasons:

- People need to grow
- We need to learn from others
- Confidence needs to be encouraged
- Change involves other people's work also
- We are not a one-man band

- I will be able to use my own skills more effectively
- We must build for the future.

The principles of delegation

Being willing to do so. Sometimes a church leader feels unable to delegate because there is no one in the congregation capable of the relevant task. That is sometimes true, but it might be an implicit confession that there has been no previous delegation to improve the capabilities of church members. The church leader may well need to adjust personal attitudes to get into a frame of mind to delegate.[34]

Releasing responsibility

> Modern delegating not only shares the work details, but also passes along much of the decision making which affects those work details. Modern delegating is not just getting others to help out on our jobs, but also giving them the authority and freedom to handle the details on their own initiative.[35]

This means that delegation is a real transfer of authority. American industrialist Andrew Carnegie said, 'The secret of success is not in doing your own work, but in recognising the right man to do it.'[36]

Having both goals and control. You need to delegate to help achieve your goals, or the goals of your organisation. You therefore need to have these known and expressed. Delegating requires giving freedom to others, but we need to ensure that within that freedom the goals are still being arrived at. We initially need to check fairly frequently that all is well while the person to whom we delegate is developing the skills needed. We can relax more subsequently as the person becomes more and more trustworthy in respect of the task given. The person delegating must describe the bounds of authority being given— the objectives, the budget, the resources, what may be done, sometimes the time involved, the reporting procedure, how to get problems solved if stuck. The person delegated to is accountable for the task given.

Following through. Delegation is not an abdication of your responsibility but a sharing of it. You still have final responsibility. It is therefore important to check fairly regularly that all is going well—once a day, once a week, or once a month according to the responsibility given, the experience and personality of the individual delegated to. Indicate, in advance, when each such check will be made, so the person knows and expects this, and does not see it as an adverse commentary on their performance. Asking people what they think helps; what they need helps more; how they would like to see it going in the future most of all. Let them grow into the task, and thus help all men become more mature in Christ. Everyone makes mistakes. A good delegator prays people will learn through the mistakes they make.

Such principles may sound fine, but, you may be asking yourself, how do you know what to delegate? Ask yourself these questions:[37]

- What keeps repeating itself in my job?
- What minor decision do I make most frequently?
- What job details take the biggest single chunks of my time?
- What parts of my job am I least qualified to handle?
- What job details do I dislike the most?
- What details in my job make me insufficiently professional?
- What details in my job make me over-technical?

Although answering such questions might help you decide what to delegate, they make one key presumption: that you have someone to delegate to. What if there is no one? I once met a vicar responsible for eleven rural churches. 'I have no lay readers, no curate, no elder, no one to help me,' he said. I wondered how strictly true that last phrase was. None of us are in churches of just ourselves! So if there are others around, ask these questions:[38]

- What kind of experience does this person need to develop his/her full value to the church?
- What details could be delegated to this person to provide variety in his/her service?
- What could be delegated that is related to what someone is already doing?

- What duties can I delegate that will provide this person with a clear objective?
- What duties have most interest for this person, and would be carried through willingly?
- What can I delegate which would give that person the right amount of challenge?
- What sequence of tasks can I delegate to this person which will give him/her a series of successes?

Before someone can accept your delegation he or she must:

- Understand what you want done (if you cannot communicate it, he/she cannot do it).
- Believe that doing it is in his/her own best interest.
- Believe it is in the interest of the church or organisation.
- Be capable because he/she has the skills.[39]

In an office where there may be several people a leader should only delegate to immediate subordinates, and not to those subordinates' juniors. One head of department may not delegate to another head of department's subordinate. Nor may an executive delegate upwards![40]

The art of delegation may be summarised as follows:

DELEGATING

Is	Is not
Giving to others responsibility for a task, and thus some authority.	Telling others to do what they are told to do.
Helping others get the skills they need to accomplish the task.	Assuming all facets of the task are initially understood.
Understanding the problems felt in coping with the responsibility.	Listening to excuses as to why the job has not been done.
Matching potential with opportunity to grow.	Giving duties to people way beyond their capability.
Trusting others to get better with experience, and so share in the decision-making process.	Wishing you had done the job in the first place.

Ensuring you show a person both why and how it is to be accomplished.

Concluding that you were stupid to give that job to that person.

Allowing errors to be made in a learning environment, giving freedom for acting as thought fit.

Pointing out all the mistakes a person has made in doing a job.

The perfect secretary

This is a special form of delegation, since your secretary, personal assistant, administrative assistant, will normally be working very closely to you, in a direct line relationship but usually without departmental responsibilities. The major attributes of a good secretary are:

- A connective memory (lateral thinker).
- An ability to get into your head, to know how you think.

It is a partnership role, which requires the executive to be trained in knowing how to take best advantage of the skills offered. Making good use of a secretary is a rare skill. She is not a status symbol, office decor, telephone call dialler or waitress—she is a colleague to help you perform better by enabling you to use your time doing those things only you can do. Here are twenty suggestions based on R. Alec Mackenzie's book *The Time Trap*:[41]

1 Your secretary should know the full range of your responsibilities and activities in your organisation. She should understand your personal goals and ambitions and how they fit in with corporate objectives.
2 You should be able to leave your office for as long as three or four weeks, confident that your business and personal affairs will be conducted responsibly and expeditiously by your secretary in your absence.
3 Your secretary should help organise your time, co-ordinate your appointments and schedules, meet your deadlines, all without nagging and pestering you. This means she needs to be a well-organised person herself.

4 She should initiate, handle and follow through projects without your having to remind her about them.

5 She should be courteous, helpful, respectful and solicitous of your business associates, visitors, clients and customers. They should speak well of her.

6 She may well need to be imaginative and creative. Can she present original ideas for your consideration? Does she suggest new ways to improve your work? Her work? Do you allow her to suggest new systems or procedures which may save your time or her time?

7 She should be resourceful, showing initiative in getting past a problem without running to you with her troubles.

8 She must be able to move paper efficiently. Can she tactfully pry loose papers and projects that have remained on your desk too long—and that other executives are waiting for? Is she able to extract data other executives are holding and that you are waiting for?

9 Her basic secretarial skills (such as filing, typing/word processing and telephone manner) need to be beyond reproach.

10 She must be calm in a crisis, and gracious when tension mounts. When the pressure is on and you lose your temper or self-composure, does she shrug it off and continue to function as well as before?

11 Does she have your absolute loyalty and confidence and do you have hers? Can you trust her with confidential information?

12 Ideally she should read widely and knowledgeably, bringing to your attention published items pertinent to your business or, perhaps, personal affairs.

13 She should be a valuable source of corporate information, obtaining facts that would be difficult, awkward or impossible for you to obtain on your own. This will help you function more effectively.

14 She ought to have a personal self-improvement programme, perhaps attending classes and lectures or participating in management-oriented programmes. She needs to learn as much as possible about your particular industry, your company, your particular job, and your customers. This can easily save time all round.

15 The best secretaries are articulate, expressing themselves well in summarising information for you, both verbally and in writing. Does your secretary give instructions clearly and precisely? Does she know how you feel about certain policies or practices, and does she communicate this to others as well as you do?

16 The ideal secretary may wish to work every day until her job is done, regardless of the hour, perhaps willingly working nights or weekends when it is necessary. But this can easily lead to an acceptance of overload, and unrealistic expectations by the executive. If extra hours are worked on an urgent job then be sure to allow time in lieu later.

17 She should be a manager in the sense that she can farm out her work to others when necessary. That is, she needs to be able to delegate, supervise and take responsibility for work not completed by herself, training and helping to train other members of your staff as appropriate.

18 A good secretary will handle routine matters and projects for you on a day-to-day basis without your intervention.

19 She should keep track of vital dates for you, dates celebrated by your boss, family and customers (anniversaries, birthdays, religious holidays, vacations, and such).

20 Good secretaries are able to do basic research for you— gather information for a report, for example, or even write a rough first draft.

The above comments assume a male executive and female secretary; the same principles govern different gender roles. If your secretary scores as many as 12–15 positive affirmations to these suggestions, you will doubtless conclude as Proverbs does in chapter 31 verse 10: 'She is far more precious than jewels.' Jewels are worth keeping—what should you do to enhance her position, encourage her person, and enable her performance to become even better? How often do you thank her? Show your appreciation? Talk to her on other than work matters? Give particular praise when an outstanding job is done? Speak well of her in front of others? Introduce her to your visitors? Invite her to join you for lunch with a visitor she knows already?

Planning visitation

As an example of applying some of the principles given earlier, let us consider how to plan a visitation programme. Ask yourself these questions:

What is your goal? What result do you expect from your visitation programme? For example, 'Twenty new people coming to church services in three months' time.'

What do you know about the houses in your area? Are they council houses or owner-occupied? Are they new, inter-war built, or older? How many are detached, semis, terraced or town houses? Are those who live in them mostly older folk, or marrieds with young families? Is there an area where a particularly high density of, say, Jews live? or black people? or Mormons?

What helps do you have for your visitation? What literature is available? Is there a film or special service you can invite people to? (One church used James Dobson's films on the family to attract people in.) Who can help you in your visiting? Could students in their vacation?

What hindrances or problems do you have? Do people not like opening the door at night? Do you speak the language? Can single women call safely? Are Jehovah's Witnesses active nearby? What training is needed? Who can best do it, and when?

What plans do you have? List all the roads and number of houses in each. Pray over them; walk round them like Nehemiah. One church deliberately set itself to do this and wrote to people in the street beforehand inviting them to indicate anything for which they specially wished prayer. Several months later people wondered why there were so few burglaries in their area. The church leader knew!

What detailed plans have been made? Specify the number of houses to be called on each week. Who will do which houses? What is the best method of contact—knocking on the door or just delivering a tract, magazine, invitation? Have you enough material? Decide how to handle requests for the minister to call.

Has the visitation form been completed? A specimen one is given below. These all need to be kept by the visitation secretary who will be responsible for initiating any actions required for liaison with others, reporting to the minister, informing the Sunday school, and so on.

Have you reviewed your progress? It is worth assessing your manner of working and your results every three months.

Visitation Record

STREET: Alpha Road					
No.	Date leaflet delivered	Called? Date	Householder's name	Comments	Action
2	3 March	No answer			
4	3 March	3 March	Smith	3 children, oldest 10	Invite Sunday school
6a	3 March	No answer			
6b	3 March	Couldn't find front door			
8	3 March	No answer			
10	4 March	4 March	Ruaja	1 child, Buddhists	
12	4 March	No answer			
14	4 March	Fierce dog		Didn't go near house	
16	6 March	No answer			
18a	6 March	6 March 8 March	Llewellyn	Shift worker on nights Second call: very friendly	Call again 5 pm Invite Easter Sunday

Maximising travel opportunities

Most Christian leaders travel at times, by road or air. How can we make the most effective use of our time on these occasions?[42]

By car. It is always useful to take a cassette player with you if you do not already have one in your car. Use it to listen to things you otherwise do not have time for, a seminar or talk, or special music. Perhaps have someone dictate a paper on to a cassette for you to listen to.

Often thoughts come as you travel which you want to record. Use a clip-on mike to dictate ideas or correspondence. This often has the calming effect of knowing you are making good use of your time and thus driving more carefully. Pray at red lights rather than getting frustrated! Take some spare reading matter with you and keep it in easy reach in case you hit a major motorway holdup.

By train. Take time to read or work on papers. Select items of work which require a minimum of writing since, although you may be able to write in a moving train, someone else may have to transcribe it! Have some small items to read on the underground.

By air. Try to combine as many visits as possible, as it is invariably cheaper that way. To whom could you make a friendship phone call? Can you book all your appointments ahead of time? Create a standard checklist of items you need to take. Plan the reading you want to do, the book you always wanted to read. Carry self-addressed envelopes to mail notes and letters home. Take small reading items for airport lounges.

This chapter has given you ten tools to help in your fight for time. Eight of them relate to your desk, but as someone once said, 'A desk is a dangerous place from which to view the world.' Ross Perot, the entrepreneurial founder of EDS and later of the Italian car industry, says, 'My first message is: listen, listen, listen to the people who do the work.'

One of Edward Deming's key insights is that 94 per cent of the problems in organisations are general problems (bad systems), and only 6 per cent are specific problems (bad people).

Many leaders misinterpret such data. The flaw in their thinking is in supposing that if they then correct the structure and systems (programmes), the problems with people (programmers) go away. The reverse is actually true—if you correct the 6 per cent first, the other problems will largely go away. Unless you work on the 6 per cent in significant ways, you can't work on the 94 per cent in significant ways, only in cosmetic ways. And you will soon revert to old ways.

Why? Because people are the programmers, and they use systems and structure as the outward expressions of their own character and competence. Strategy, structure and systems are the 'software' programmes written by your programmers, your people.[43]

So in your fight for time, never forget the people who make your world go round.

Summary

- Your diary is essentially a planning instrument, and must be able to be shared. Use it to give you time to plan.
- Successful meetings require advance work and good chairing.
- Interruptions to serious work should be allowed only in crises.
- Limit your availability.
- The telephone is an extension of your personality—use it thoughtfully, carefully, pleasantly.
- Procrastination afflicts us all from time to time. Plan your way through. Know what you are not doing. Be positive in outlook.
- Retrieving notes afterwards requires indexing as you take them.
- Delegating is both an art and science. You only develop your skill at it with practice.
- A perfect secretary is worth her weight in gold—so do your best to keep her happy and secure.
- The best visitation is thoroughly planned, with clear expectation, delegation and application.
- Always use travelling time to the best advantage.

7

TIME TO STAND AND STARE—
WHAT ME?

Fitting the Time Jigsaw Together

What is this life if, full of care
We have no time to stand and stare?

In somewhat desperate circumstances, C.P. Scott took over the
then *Manchester Guardian*. But he was a journalist in his heart
and disliked slanting the news to fit his own opinions, a practice
not common among newspaper owners of that time—or since.
So he gave his reporters a free hand, and reporters, respecting
this, would serve him well. The economics of the paper meant
moderate wages, and, although he was the owner of the paper,
he personally took only a modest salary and refused to have a
company car.

About half past two one morning he was pushing his bicycle
up a hill on the outskirts of Manchester, quite slowly as he was
in his early seventies. Suddenly a policeman appeared.

'And where are you going at this hour of the night?'

'I'm going home.'

'And what have you been doing?'

'Working.'

'Working! Where?'

He told him.

'The *Guardian*! They ought to be ashamed of themselves,
working an old chap like you!'[1]

Yes, people will work when they are motivated so to do.
Jesus did. As Martyn Dunning and Lance Pierson point out in
an *Adminisheet*,[2] Jesus *kept long hours*. On the Sabbath day
recorded in Mark 1:21–34, we find Him teaching, exorcising
and healing well into the night. Yet the following morning He

rose 'a great while before day' to pray. After feeding the five thousand, He went to pray and then met the disciples in the early hours of the morning on the middle of Lake Galilee, where He had walked.

Jesus missed meals, saying to the disciples after talking to the Samaritan woman that He had food which they did not know. He spent forty days in the wilderness, tempted to turn stones into bread. But Jesus *accomplished an enormous amount*. He visited many of the villages in the Capernaum neighbourhood, went to the Decapolis, walked to Caesarea Philippi in the foothills of Mount Hermon, spoke in Jerusalem, ministered in Judea, and so filled His three years that John doubted whether the world could contain an account of everything Jesus did[3].[4]

Motivation

But what are we motivated for? To serve? To preach? To counsel? To guide? To plan? The answer is 'Yes', perhaps to all these, and in several other areas also. A group of Christian leaders at a MARC Europe seminar were asked to draw up a list of their key difficulties. Here is that list. With how many would you identify?

Lack of a realistic feeling for the future ☐

Reliance on past performance rather than present credibility ☐

Unerring knack of drawing the wrong conclusions from the facts ☐

Inability to draw up sensible timetables ☐

Lack of accurate understanding of people's feelings ☐

Inability to communicate enthusiastically ☐

Unwillingness to take advantage of the strategic opportunity (that is, unwilling to risk) ☐

Loss of a sense of finesse ☐

Lack of clear policy when needed ☐

Being logical rather than wise ☐

What, then, are some of the key problems that have to be solved in the time jigsaw that everyone faces? Frequently many of the difficulties relate to our use of time.

We often *fail to persevere*. Why do so many pastors find goal setting difficult? Because they come to their church 'without the determination to stay there long enough to make it succeed'.[5] Wrote C.S. Lewis's Screwtape devil to his junior, Wormwood:

> You see it is so hard for these creatures to *persevere*. The routine of adversity, the gradual decay of youthful loves and youthful hopes, the quiet despair (hardly felt as pain)...the drabness which we create in their lives, and the inarticulate resentment...provides admirable opportunities of wearing out a Soul by attrition.[6]

We often *fail to hope*. Hope accepts tragedy with courage. The father of American civil rights leader, Martin Luther King, had to endure not only his son's assassination but his wife's murder too. But he continued his work for the Lord. When speaking about the church he said, 'The business of the church is to give everyone a sense of belonging.' His hope was not in this world but in the next where every tear will be wiped away and every broken fence be mended.[7] We properly give love the highest place, but hope too is a major component of Paul's vital triumvirate, and we must not neglect it. How do you grow in hope? In part, by knowing your purpose. God has a job for you to do that no one else can.

We often *fail to plan*. What is it that you are about? Neil Strait, a district superintendent in the Church of the Nazarene, asks, 'What should the finished project look like? What are the goals? You must know the destination before the journey begins. The objective, purpose and reasons must be clearly in mind. If this is not so, ideas along the way will interrupt the project.'[8] Part of our failure to plan is a failure to repent of our lack of planning. The International Evangelical Lutheran Church in Helsinki, Finland, regularly prays, 'O Lord, forgive what we have been. Amend what we are. Direct what we shall be, that we may delight in your will and walk in your ways.'

I woke up early this morning,
and paused before entering the day;
I had so much to accomplish
that I had to take time to pray.[9]

Turning failure into success

How do we turn our failures, especially our time failures, into success? David left his native Nottingham and trained as a vet. By the age of thirty he was already happy, secure and successful in his professional practice in Edinburgh. But then he heard God's call to leave all that for a new and unpredictable sphere of service.

So David swapped the care of pets in Edinburgh for the care of people in Ealing. After pastoral training, he started his new life as a minister in a church celebrating its centenary in the hurly-burly of a cosmopolitan London suburb. The church there had 200 members.

But alas, David found himself in a situation all too common among today's Christian leaders. It was not the pastoring which gave him his biggest problems. It was the demands of the sheer paperwork and management skills needed to run what amounted to a small business.

'I had had no experience at all of that sort of thing. It was completely mystifying,' he confessed. And David sank. Burdened by administration, he could not concentrate on the heart of the clear task to which God had called him—to make disciples. He had to take an extended holiday, utterly exhausted. Then he spotted a brochure for a MARC Europe course, 'The Effective Use of Time'. After attending the course he wrote to us.

It was an absolute eye-opener. I was most impressed by the way a biblical reason was given for everything. We were shown how the management ideas emerged from biblical understanding. It has made an amazing difference to my ministry and my personal life. Now I know how to set priorities and goals and work towards them—and each department in the church is doing the same. I can avoid the accumulation of paperwork which used to swamp me. I have reorganised my office, and my desk is empty at weekends. I get through much more in less time.

This is very important in the church, as membership is growing, and some are training for mission. I actually feel fresh, invigorated, and have a peace about my work.

I came back full of new ideas and with a fresh approach that has made a lot of difference. I feel in control of the work—and that's a liberating experience.

I am amazed how basic some of the information was— silly things, really, like not letting work accumulate and only reading letters once, when you answer them. Now I file things in an Action file and get through them a lot quicker in one go.

I have a secretary and realised that I was not using her well at all. Many of the things I was taught have enabled me to make her work easier and we get through much more in much less time. I even have time to write letters of appreciation—something I rarely did before.

The small office in which he works at the back of the church bears evidence of the renewed spirit. A filing cabinet has been manhandled across the room nearer to the desk. 'I realised that every time I wanted a paper I had to walk across the room. Moving the cabinet nearer was so obvious—but I wouldn't have thought about it without that course.'

'After I got back from the course, I overheard a deacon say "We have a new minister!" He meant me!'

Other examples

Like our fingerprints, each of us is unique in the way we use time. William Carey gives us the pattern of ordered, sheer hard work. An extract from his diary is given in Appendix 1. Another workaholic, this time an American Congregational minister, gives her reactions to pressure in Appendix 2. These are *not* held up for emulation.

Summary

This book has looked at the problems inherent in the fight for time. You can win by acting on its five key principles. Put up your hand in front of you, and imagine five letters painted one on each fingernail, like this:

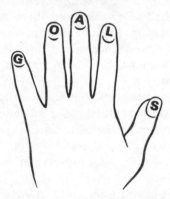

Fig 16: GOALS are essential

Use this simple mnemonic in order to gain the time you need.

G = *set Goals*. What is it you actually want to accomplish? What is your mission in life? What do you wish to see happen this year, this month? Write it down, make a note so that you begin to know where you are going. Aim specifically, realistically, measurably. It can be done!

O = *handle paper Once only*. All of us have plenty of reports, correspondence and other paperwork. The secret of success in the paper war is to handle each individual item as infrequently as possible, and ideally once only. Take action on the piece of paper as it comes; do not waste time reading it in detail now; have a plan of action for controlling your incoming paper and stick to it.

A = *'A' priorities first*. The purpose of setting priorities is so that you can work to them once identified. There is no point in knowing what you should be doing and doing something else.

We need bullseye prioritisers, as the expression in *'Christian' England*[10] puts it, and the story told there is worth repeating.

One September day in San Antonio, Texas, when the temperature stood at 99°F (37°C), a baby girl was accidentally locked inside a parked car by her aunt. The mother and aunt ran round the car frantically while a neighbour tried to unlock the door with a coat hanger. Soon the infant was turning purple and had foam on her mouth when Fred, a lorry driver, arrived on the scene. He grabbed a hammer and smashed the back window and set the girl free. Was he thanked? 'The lady was mad at me because I broke the window. I just thought—What's more important—the baby or the window?' What's your bullseye priority?

L = *List jobs daily.* You must know your long-term goals, but also need to plan your activities today as far as possible. The unexpected may still happen, but at least you have the scaffolding of what you intended to do to hold you in place and enable you still to build what you may from this day's work. There is only one today—and that is today! So make the most of it!

The S is probably the most important letter.

S = *Start now.* It is easy to read a book on time management but if that is all you do it will not help you. Start today to put some of these ideas, concepts, suggestions into practice. Do not wait till tomorrow. Write below three things that you will aim to do as a result of reading this book:

1 _____

2 _____

3 _____

Ray Horrocks, along with Sir Michael Edwardes and David Andrews, was one of the three men at the top of British Leyland as it was making a tense recovery in the hectic days in 1981 and 1982. On the wall in Ray's office there was a picture of two seagulls in flight, and underneath an inscription translated from Virgil:

Fig 17: 'They can, because they think they can'

Precisely so! You can if you think you can. The Lord asked Abraham, 'Is anything too hard for the Lord?'[11] The angel Gabriel said to Mary, 'With God nothing will be impossible.'[12] Jesus said, 'All things are possible to him who believes.'[13] 'I could never become efficient,' you say. Not so! You can if you really want to. 'I cannot sort and handle all this paperwork in an effective way,' you think. Not true! You can begin to as quickly as you think you can. 'I'm not able to phone, plan, think in detail,' you argue. Never the case! Your ability to do so grows as you start. *Nothing* is impossible with God.

You can change like David, the pastor mentioned above. Paul says, 'Do you not know that in a race all the runners compete, but only one receives the prize? So run that you may obtain it.'[14] And may God bless you in your labours. They are not in vain.

TAKE TIME

Take time to think
It is the source of power.

Take time to play
It is the source of perpetual youth.

Take time to pray
It is the greatest power on earth.

Take time to love and be loved
It is a God-given privilege.

Take time to be friendly
It is the road to happiness.

Take time to laugh
It is the music of the soul.

Take time to give
It is too short a day to be selfish.

Take time to work
It is the price of success.

Anon

APPENDIX 1:
A DAY IN THE LIFE OF WILLIAM CAREY

As described in a letter from Calcutta

Fig 18: William Carey

I rose this morning at a quarter before six, read a chapter in the Hebrew Bible, and spent the time till seven in private addresses to God, and then attended family prayer with the servants in Bengali. While tea was getting ready, I read a little in Persian with a moonshi [language teacher] who was waiting when I left my bedroom; and also before breakfast a portion of the Scripture in Hindustani. The moment breakfast was over, sat down to the translation of the Ramayana from Sanskrit, with a pundit [learned Hindu expert], who was also waiting, and continued this translation till ten o'clock, at which hour I went to College and attended the duties there till between one and two o'clock. When I returned home, I examined a proof-sheet of the Bengali translation of Jeremiah, which took till dinnertime. I always, when down in Calcutta, dine at Mr Rolt's which is near. After dinner, translated, with the assistance of the chief pundit of the College, the greatest part of the eighth chapter of

Matthew into Sanskrit. This employed me till six o'clock. After six, sat down with a Telinga pundit to learn the language. At seven I began to collect a few previous thoughts into the form of a sermon, and preached at half-past seven. About forty persons present, and among them one of the Puisne Judges of the Sudder Dewany Adawlut. After sermon I got a subscription from him for five hundred rupees towards erecting our new place of worship; he is an exceedingly friendly man. Preaching was over and the congregation gone by nine o'clock. I then sat down and translated the eleventh of Ezekiel into Bengali, and this lasted till near eleven; and now I sit down to write to you.[1]

APPENDIX 2:
DON'T TELL ME TO
TAKE CARE OF MYSELF

As a pastor and a parent, I work two shifts, one at church and the second at home. At the church, I minister and administer, marry and bury, preach and pray, and in a thousand other ways, 'do church'. At home I get cards to in-laws, groceries to refrigerators, children to birthday parties, and garments to and from the dry cleaner.

Like most pastors (and parents), I have been charged with the job of caring. It's a never-ending task.

This job description joins my authority as pastor in requiring me to shoot the next person who tells me to 'take care of myself'. I know I can't continue forever to do dishes and talk on the phone simultaneously. The day will come when I won't have the energy to do my correspondence in the evening while watching television. I don't plan to go on like this forever, not wasting a moment. But until my three children are raised and/or the millennium arrives, I don't plan to take care of myself. I plan to take care of my children and my promises to God and the church.

Some people accuse me of doing too much. My mother does, as do my friends who read too many magazines on the fine art of self-care. 'Oh, my,' they all say about my three children, my full-time job, and my full calendar, 'I just don't know how you do it.'

'That's the whole point,' I reply. 'I don't do it.'

My vocation is caring, and every day I fail to fully realise it.

You don't succeed in caring; you simply do as much as you can and try to stretch your capacity.

I don't finish everything I start. For every call I make, I can think of two more I should have made. I leave the phone answering machine on for extensive periods when I am home. I cut corners. I keep sewing projects in plastic bags for years just so I can remember that I would enjoy an evening with busy hands and an empty mind.

I triage my desk every few months and throw out piles of unanswered mail. Every week I do the same with the telephone list. If the stack of calls to return goes over thirty by Friday, I declare an emergency. Then I pick the five or so who really need a reply and lose the rest of the pink slips. Then I forgive myself for not 'doing it'.

Am I proud of my tendency to overextend? You bet. I don't think being overextended is the sin the self-care movement purports it to be. Rather I am inclined to locate sin in self-care, in being careful not to get tired, in focusing on the limits rather than the possibilities in my energy.

Do I get tired? Yes. Frequently. Worse—and this really makes my New Age friends cluck—I even get sick. Colds, the flu, minor aches, and once a serious illness. Yet even after that illness, once I learned I wasn't going to die tomorrow (a fear I indulged quite thoroughly), I went back to my old bad habit of filling up the appointment book and trying to have fun at the same time.

The ability to care does not mean that you don't have fun or that you don't relax. I find time to be quiet and prayerful each day. I find time to write almost as often. I get to my garden for several good sessions of earth a week. And I have an active social life. People seem to fear caring for others because it threatens these things. The threat is mental not actual.

So why am I going to shoot the next person who advises me to take care of myself? Why this long, defensive description of my lifestyle? The reason is simple. I feel like I am under attack, being shot at by some new and sinister enemy, whose cover is 'Take Care of Yourself'. But his real purpose is to stifle my ministry, to keep me from having the fun of making my own contributions to the world, and to keep me from making other people uncomfortable.

Rather than backing off our full schedules, I think we should invite other people to join us in full-throttle caring. Caring goes wrong when I carry all the responsibility for it. It safely expands if I do it publicly, freely inviting others to join me in caring. Choosing a full life means being busy.

Caring, by its very nature, grows. Try to care well for a few, and if you succeed, you will find more people calling your name. Welcome one homeless person to your congregation and see what happens.

I remember the head of a local welfare agency saying that he didn't want to provide good service to his clients because that would only increase the demand. What a complex excuse for not caring.

Being busy is not all that bad. Right now I actively choose ministry and children and friends and quiet. That's how I take care of myself.

I tell people: 'If the chaos of my overbooked life is getting to you, or if you think my contribution has become haggard, by all means ask me to rest. I will appreciate your concern, deeply. I don't want to look like an overdeveloped suburb any more than you want to look at one. I want the plantings around my house to look mature; I want space left over. I need margins as much as anyone.

'If you think I'm looking crowded, say so. But don't ask me to do less, and don't accuse me of "not taking care of myself". That I simply don't plan to do.'[2]

APPENDIX 3:
JOB DESCRIPTION OF
AN ANGLICAN VICAR

This job description assumes that six committees exist, covering the key ministries of the local church: committees for discipleship, worship, mission, service, evangelism and fellowship. Where these do not exist, modifications will obviously be necessary. Sometimes the committee may be just one person to whom relevant duties and responsibilities can be delegated.

Basic goal

With the help of the Holy Spirit, to grow into the likeness of Jesus, through prayer, the study of the Scriptures, and the practice of the Christian faith so that the message of reconciliation is heard by members of X Church, by the parishioners and by others coming within reach, and that every opportunity is provided for their spiritual and social growth and ministry.

To co-operate with the Parochial Church Council or deacons in promoting the whole mission of the church, pastoral, evangelical, social and ecumenical.

Responsibilities

1   *To preach on the Lord's Day* when the church assembles and to invite other gifted people to share this work;

To be responsible for mid-week teaching centrally or in house groups.

To ensure that the ministry of the word of God is building

the church and to note those with a preaching/teaching gift and encourage the development and exercise of those gifts.

To take note of the advice of the discipleship committee.

2 *To preside at worship and over the sacraments,* or make appropriate arrangements when absent.

To be the focus of the unity of the church.

To ensure that all the necessary gifts for a worshipping community are developed and used.

To appoint Readers, after consultation with the PCC, to assist in the conduct of worship and such other duties as they feel may be appropriately requested.

To say the daily office with the staff and any other leaders who can be present, and to give adequate time for private intercession for the people and for the development of his personal devotional time.

To take note of the advice of the worship committee.

3 *To exercise the pastoral ministry* that is appropriate for an ordained man, for which he has been given specific authority.

To give time to crisis visiting.

To ensure that regular pastoral care is given to the whole congregation; and to use house group leaders and other suitable persons to this end.

To take note of the advice of the fellowship committee.

4 *To lead the church in mission,* taking note of the advice of the missionary, service and discipleship and evangelism committees, and to this end to ensure that:

evangelism is carried out by appropriate means

missionary interest is deepened

social justice and service are understood and worked out by the congregation

leadership gifts appropriate to mission are discovered and encouraged.

5 *To appoint the curate* after close consultation with the church wardens and committee chair persons.

To be responsible, with the diocesan authorities, for the training of the curate and to ensure that he develops an all-round ministry and strengthens his special gifts by delegating to him specific duties, and to ensure that the rules for pay and conditions are strictly observed.

6 *To appoint two church wardens* in consultation with the vestry meeting, and to share with the church wardens in the oversight of the church, so that there are full consultations, communication and carefully prepared decisions through the committees.

To chair the annual parochial and vestry meetings, unless he decides that the lay chairman of the PCC should so act.

To act an an ex-officio member of all church committees, to be the chairman of the PCC unless he chooses to delegate it, and to act as a member of the Deanery Synod and Chapter.

To appoint officials such as the organist, choirmaster, honorary curate, and the leaders of the singing group, drama group, cameo, women's fellowship and house groups after consultation with the church wardens.

To hold a weekly staff meeting attended by the curate (if any) and any other full-time member of staff.

To delegate to his secretary the typing of letters and reports on the equipment provided, the answering of the phone, responsibility for his diary, filing, and the servicing of the church wardens, chairpersons, curate and treasurer.

To give time to encourage and develop the six chairpersons in their work.

To appoint chairpersons (in close consultation with the church wardens) who will lead the committees responsible for the church's work, and to meet with them, and any others invited, to discuss the life of the church at least once a month.

7 *To avail himself of training* and of conferences and to accept outside engagements and ministry so long as his work at X Church does not suffer.

Appointed by: The Bishop of Y, on the advice of the patrons and the agreement of the church wardens.

Responsible to: God the Father, God the Son and God the Holy Spirit through the Bishop of Y.

APPENDIX 4:
FILING SYSTEMS

It may be helpful to give fuller details of two filing systems. That of Canon Michael Saward was introduced in Chapter 5 (see page 139). His eight major subdivisions are as follows:

00-09 The Church
10-19 The Scriptures
20-29 Christian Doctrine
30-39 The Church's Public Ministry
40-49 Church Auxiliaries and Agencies
50-59 Parochial Administration
60-69 Personal and Family Matters
70-79 General Subjects

Each of these can be sub-divided further, so that, for example, a breakdown of Church Auxiliaries and Agencies, is:

40 Parish Fellowship
41 Younger Children's Work
42 Bible Classes
43 Children's Clubs
44 Youth Work
45 Adult Organisations
46 Parish Missionary Interest
47 Bookstall and Library
48 Church Social Clubs

49   Local Secular Organisations and Personalities

Each of these also can be subdivided further, so that, for example, a breakdown of, say, No 42—Bible Classes, is:

42.0   General
42.1   National Organisations
42.2   Teachers
42.3   Syllabus
42.4   Equipment
42.5   Members
42.6   Camps
42.7   Special Events

and each of these may be further subdivided as necessary.

For those wanting details of this system, contact Canon Michael Saward BA, The Chapter House, St Paul's Church Yard, London, EC4M 8AD.

At MARC Europe we use a FACTS (Files And Correspondence Tracing System) system. This allocates a basic four digit number to every file, with one or two letters in front and the option of extra numbers at the end. The first digit of the four indicates the major category as follows:

0   Reference
1   Denominational handbook
2   Bible and biblical exposition
3   Christian mission
4   Church statistics
5   Secular statistics
6   Management and leadership
7   Political, geographical and economic areas
8   MARC Europe contacts and meetings
9   Audio-visual materials and artwork

Two further digits provide a country designation. Thus 6491 could be the basic reference number for 'Effective Use of Time' seminars, where the 6 denotes that it is in the leadership and management category (which also carries a colour code), the 49 denotes the United Kingdom, and 1 is a sequential number since this was our first one-day seminar. Each such number can carry two letters in front of it, one to depict the department responsible for that file (T for training in this case) and the second letter for where it is filed (F for filing cabinet, L for library, and so on). Thus TF6491 might be the general descripton for the EUT programme, indicating the file was a training department file, kept in their filing cabinet. TF6491/93 covers the 1993 programme. TL6491/89 shows that the 1989 programme, no longer needed, is kept in the library. TF6461/93 is our Finnish programme (46 = Finland) in 1993.

In fact our system is slightly more sophisticated. We do not have a file labelled 'Effective Use of Time' (EUT), for example—it is too general. Instead we have titles such as: EUT–1993 Programme; EUT–Evaluation; EUT–Location; EUT–Speakers; EUT–Handout revisions; EUT–Enquiries; EUT Handout–Translation into Finnish; EUT Handout–Translation into Hebrew, and so on. If necessary these are broken down further, such as EUT–Evaluation 1984–1988; EUT–Evaluation 1989–1993, EUT–Evaluation–Strategy implications, and so on.

We index 'Effective Use of Time' under E in our associated alphabetical list, but also index Programme–EUT. Finland is also indexed, and we might index Evaluation and Handout, for example, too, depending on how important these were considered to be.

APPENDIX 5:
BIBLIOGRAPHY

Austin, Bruce. *Time, The Essence*. British Institute of Management: London, 1979.

A manager's work book for using time effectively, based on the use of one's diary, and on a detailed analysis of it, in two volumes with blank forms.

Barna, George. *How To Find Your Church*, World Wide Publications: Minneapolis, 1989.

A helpful book for thinking through issues.

Battersby, Albert. *Mathematics in Management*. Penguin: Middlesex, 1968.

Chapter 2 is very helpful on PERT diagrams and their compilation.

Beveridge, W.E. *Managing the Church*. SCM: London, 1971.

Structures and objectives in the church from a lecturer with business and industrial experience.

Brierley, Peter W. *Vision Building*, MARC Europe and Hodder & Stoughton, 1989.

Finding your vision as an individual or organisation, and planning to make it work.

Cormack, David. *Seconds Away!* Fifteen rounds in the fight for effective use of time. MARC Europe, 1986.

Vision building, targets, priorities, strategy, progress, energy, with a mass of practical exercises.

Culligan, Matthew J., Deakins, Suzanne, Young, Arthur H. *Back-to-Basics Management: The Lost Craft of Leader-*

ship. Gower: Aldershot, Hants, 1983.
Managing time, along with change, motivation, delegation, leadership and goal setting.

Dayton, Edward R. *God's Purpose/Man's Plans*. MARC: Monrovia, California, USA, 1971.
A work book on understanding God's purposes, becoming part of his planning, problem solving.

Dayton, Edward R. *Tools for Time Management*, Zondervan Publishing House: Grand Rapids, Michigan, USA, 1978.
Christian perspectives on managing priorities.

Dayton, Edward R. and Engstrom, Ted W. *Managing Your Time*. Seminar handout, MARC: Monrovia, California, USA, 1976. (Available from MARC Europe.)
Time analysis, goals, and strategy for living.

Dayton, Edward R. and Engstrom, Ted W. *Strategy for Living*. Regal Books: USA, 1976.
Goals, priorities, planning the process of living. Accompanied by a work book.

Dayton, Edward R. and Engstrom, Ted W. *Strategy for Leadership*. Fleming H. Revell: Old Tappan, New Jersey, USA, 1979.
Planning, activating, motivating, evaluating with emphasis on the practical.

Dayton, Edward R. and Engstrom, Ted W. *The Best Way to Plan Your Day*. Pocket guide. Tyndale House Publishers: Wheaton, Illinois, USA, 1989. (Available through Scripture Press, Amersham.)
Brief practical guide to goal setting, priorities, planning and living.

Dayton, Edward R and Fraser, David A. *Planning Strategies for World Evangelisation* (Revised edition) William B. Eerdman Publishing Company: Grand Rapids, Michigan, 1990.

Engstrom, Ted W. and Dayton, Edward R. *The Christian Executive*. Word Books: Waco, Texas, USA, 1979.
Practical guide for Christians in management positions, leaders of Christian organisations, pastors and other Christian workers, putting in book form early issues of the popular *Christian Leadership Letters*.

Engstrom, Ted W. and Mackenzie, R. Alec. *Managing Your Time*. Practical guidelines on the effective use of time. Zondervan Publishing House: Grand Rapids, Michigan, USA, 1967.

Work, time and leisure, and focusing on how to manage yourself.

Ferner, Jack D. *Successful Time Management*. A self-teaching guide. John Wiley & Sons Inc: New York, USA, 1980.

Self-assessment guide for action, with planning schedules, and examples. Covers handling interruptions, effective delegating, improving meetings, and procrastination. Comes with a helpful leader's guide.

Gibbs, Eddie. *Followed or Pushed?* MARC Europe: London, 1987.

Looks at leadership issues, but has a valuable section on job descriptions.

Haggai, John. *Lead On!* Word Books; Waco, Texas.

Has three useful chapters on vision, goal setting and energy.

Jay, Anthony. *How to Run a Meeting*. Video Arts: London, 1974.

A look at successful and disastrous meetings, and how to make more of the latter like the former.

Jensen, Phillip D. and Payne, Tony. *Fellow Workers*. St Matthias Press: New South Wales, 1989.

Particularly useful chapters on meetings and decision making.

Kuhrt, Gordon W. *Handbook for Council and Committee Members*. Mowbray: Oxford, 1985.

An excellent overview of the responsibilities, duties and functions of belonging to a committee.

Laird, Donald A. and Laird, Eleanor C. *The Techniques of Delegating*. McGraw-Hill: New York, USA, 1957. (Now out of print.)

Sociological, psychological and team-building aspects of delegation.

Locke, M. *How to Run Committees and Meetings*. Macmillan: London, 1980.

A helpful guide to both.

Macaulay, Steve. *Easing the Pressure*. An A-Z of managing your time and stress.
Corporate Management Training: BBC, 1989.
Covers most perspectives of time management, and stress problems in a useful alphabetical order.

McClung, Sally. *Where will I find the time?* Kingsway: Eastbourne, 1988; with Youth With A Mission.
A leader's wife talks practically about building time for marriage, family, friends, life, work, fun and healing.

Rush, Myron. *Burnout*. Scripture Press: Amersham-on-the-Hill, Bucks, 1989.

NOTES

1: I DON'T HAVE ANY SPARE TIME

1 Roger Devlin, 'Tulsa Tribune', quoted in *Reader's Digest* (May 1990), p 139.
2 Oswald C.J. Hoffman, sermon 'The Gift of Time'.
3 Katherine Chandler, *Reader's Digest* desk calendar, 1990.
4 David Cormack, *Seconds Away* (MARC Europe, 1985).
5 Rowland Croucher, 'Stress and Spirituality' seminar, Holland, October 1990.
6 Helmut Schmidt, quoted in *International Management* (May 1990), p 11.
7 Proverbs 29:18.
8 Rowland Croucher, *Still Waters, Deep Waters* (Albatross, 1987), p 246.
9 Genesis 5:24.
10 Deuteronomy 34:10.
11 2 Samuel 1:23.
12 2 Kings 23:25.
13 2 Chronicles 21:16,20.
14 Isaiah 41:8.
15 Revelation 2:13.
16 Peter H. Brierley, *Vision Building* (MARC Europe and Hodder & Stoughton: London, 1989), p 26.
17 Edward R. Dayton, 'How to Get Where You're Going', *Christian Leadership Letter* (September 1987).

18 Robert Schuller, *Your Church Has a Fantastic Future* (Regal Books, 1986).
19 Mark Silversides, strategy summary of seminar, 1990.
20 Myron Rush, *The New Leader* (Victor Books, Scripture Press, 1989), p 111.
21 1 Corinthians 13:11.
22 Brierley, *op cit*, pp 186–188.
23 Jack Hayford, 'Why I Don't Set Goals', *Leadership* (Winter 1984), p 47.
24 Mark 2:5.
25 Matthew 10:5.
26 2 Corinthians 10:13.
27 Deuteronomy 7:22.
28 1 Peter 4:10.
29 Rush, *op cit*, p 103.
30 Based on Dayton, *op cit*, p 2.
31 Philippians 3:13.
32 Matthew 5:48.
33 Ephesians 2:10.

2: I DON'T HAVE ENOUGH TIME

1 James Woudhysen, *Management Today* (November 1989), p 38.
2 John 19:30.
3 Janice Wise, 'Needed: Grace for Growing Old', *Decision* (July/August 1990).
4 Peter W. Brierley, *Vision Building* (MARC Europe and Hodder & Stoughton: London, 1989), Chapter 4.
5 David Cormack, 'Effective Use of Time', seminar, MARC Europe, 1985.
6 Interview with Carl George, in 'Behind the Firehouse Syndrome', *Leadership* (Winter 1985), p 14.
7 *Ibid*.
8 *Ibid*.
9 Gordon MacDonald, *Restoring Your Spiritual Passion* (Highland Books: Crowborough, East Sussex, 1986).
10 Matthew 5:24.
11 Matthew 6:33.

12 Matthew 7:5.
13 Matthew 22:38.
14 Luke 17:25.
15 2 Corinthians 8:12.
16 Ephesians 6:2.
17 1 Timothy 5:4.
18 Philip D. Harvey and James D. Snyder, 'Charities Need a Bottom Line Too', *Harvard Business Review* (January/February 1987), p 14.
19 *Leaders Under Pressure*, MARC Europe Research Report, Monograph 37, (1991), p 19.
20 Edward R. Dayton, ' "What Next?" Establishing Priorities', *Christian Leadership Letter* (March 1973).
21 Bob McCelloud, World Vision of Canada, personal conversation, August 1990.
22 Alan Flavelle, 'The Church—Today and Tomorrow', *Journal of the Irish Christian Study Centre*, Vol 2 (1984): p 28.
23 'Little Things Mean A Lot', *Christopher News Notes, New York*, No 323 (1989).
24 Alan Lakein, *How to get control of your time and your life* (Signet Books: USA, 1973).
25 Myron Rush, *Burnout* (Scripture Press, 1989), p 13.
26 Quoted in *Reader's Digest* (August 1990): p 122.
27 Kay Yow, 'I Reached a Dream', *Decision* (February 1990), p 5.
28 Edward R. Dayton, *Tools for Time Management* (Zondervan: Michigan, USA, 1974), p 51.
29 John Stott, at 150th anniversary celebration of All Souls Church, London, November 1974.
30 Paul Beasley-Murray, *Dynamic Leadership* (MARC, 1989), pp 65–67.
31 'Towards extending the Church's influence—anywhere', reproduced in *The Canadian C.S. Lewis Journal*, No 72 (Autumn 1990), p 9.
32 Quoted in Sally McClung, *Where will I find the time?* (Kingsway, 1988).
33 Bill Hybels, *Too Busy Not to Pray* (IVP: Nottingham, 1988).

3: I DON'T HAVE TIME TO WORK IT OUT

1 Jeremiah 29:11.
2 Matthew J. Culligan et al, *Back to Basics Management* (Gower, 1983), p 70.
3 Ted W. Engstrom and R. Alec Mackenzie, *Managing Your Time* (Zondervan: Michigan, USA, 1979), p 111.
4 Proverbs 13:19 (Living Bible).
5 Edward R. Dayton, 'Planning: Part 1', *Christian Leadership Letter* (May 1973).
6 Graeme Irvine, opening the World Vision Directors' Conference, Germany, 8 May 1990.
7 Robert Waterman, *The Renewal Factor* (Bantam Books, 1988), p 47.
8 David Cormack, *Seconds Away* (MARC Europe: London, 1986), pp 71f. See also Bryn Hughes, handout for 'Effective Use of Time' seminar, 1989, pp 33f.
9 Edward R. Dayton, *Tools for Time Management* (Zondervan: Michigan, USA, 1978), p 127.
10 A. Orton, *Learning Mathematics: Issues, Theory and Classroom Practice* (Cassell: London), p 35.
11 Edward R. Dayton and Ted W. Engstrom, *The Best Way to Plan Your Day* (Tyndale House: Illinois, USA, 1989), pp 40f.
12 Peter W. Brierley, *Vision Building* (MARC Europe and Hodder & Stoughton: London, 1989), Chapter 5.
13 Luke 14:28.
14 Edward R. Dayton and Ted W. Engstrom, *Strategy for Leadership* (Revell: New Jersey, USA, 1979).
15 *Glossary of Management Techniques* (HM Treasury, 1967), pp 13f.
16 Edward R. Dayton and David A. Fraser, *Planning Strategies for World Evangelisation* (Wm Eerdmans: Grand Rapids, Michigan, USA; and MARC International: California, USA, revised edition 1990), p 298.
17 Edward R. Dayton, *God's Purpose/Man's Plans* (MARC International: California, USA, 1982).
18 Ted W. Engstrom and Edward R. Dayton, *The Christian Executive* (Ward: Texas, USA, 1979), p 120.
19 Quoted in *Leadership* (Spring 1990), p 27.

20 Edward R. Dayton, *Managing Your Time*, seminar manual, 1977, p 71.
21 Simon and Schuster, 'As I am', quoted in *Reader's Digest* (May 1990), p 27.
22 Isaiah 40:3, 4.
23 Graeme Irvine, in internal paper of World Vision, 1976.
24 Lee Iacocca, *Talking Straight* (Sidgwick and Jackson: London, 1988).
25 Brierley, *op cit*, pp 167f.
26 *Ibid*, pp 191f.
27 Chief Executive Officers (of evangelical mission organisations) Conference, 1985.
28 David Cormack, 'Effective Use of Time' seminar, MARC Europe, 1986.
29 Stephen Gaukroger, *Leadership Today* (October 1987), p 31; and also quoted in Brierley, *op cit*, p 163.
30 Dayton, *Managing Your Time*, p 6.
31 1 Thessalonians 5:24.

4: I DON'T THINK IT WILL WORK

1 Tom Houston, International Affairs Committee Working Group, World Vision International, Los Angeles, USA, August 1988.
2 Mark 14:5.
3 George Barna, *How to Find Your Church* (World Wide Publications: Minneapolis, USA, 1989), p 27.
4 *Ibid*.
5 *Ibid*, p 39.
6 The figures are $8 \times 7 = 56$ for friendliness, $7 \times 9 = 63$ for a good Sunday school, $8 \times 7 = 56$ for helping non-Christians, $7 \times 8 = 56$ for service, $9 \times 10 = 90$ for theological basis and $9 \times 6 = 54$ for travel. $56 + 63 + 56 + 56 + 90 + 54 = 375$. $375 \div 47 = 7.9787$, or 8.0 to one decimal place.
7 Alan Wenban-Smith of Segal Quince Wickstead Ltd to the Council of BIM, 27 September 1990.
8 Peter W. Brierley, *'Christian' England* (MARC Europe, 1991), maps at the end of the book.

9 Eddie Gibbs, *Followed or Pushed?* (MARC Europe, 1987), p 124.
10 Proverbs 15:22.
11 Proverbs 21:5.
12 C. Collins, *Reader's Digest* desk calendar and appointments book, 1990.
13 Robert Horton, advertising leaflet of the BIM, 1990.
14 Quoted in Robert Waterman, *The Renewal Factor* (Bantam Books, 1988), p 49.
15 *Ibid*, p 51.
16 *Ibid*, pp 52–53.
17 Ray L. Willsmer, *The Basic Arts of Marketing* (Business Books, Hutchinson, 1984), p 149.

5: I DON'T HAVE TIME TO ANSWER THAT

1 Genesis 1:4,12,18,25,31.
2 *Leadership* (Spring 1990), p 95.
3 British and Foreign Bible Society survey, May 1980, quoted with permission.
4 Quoted in *Reader's Digest* (February 1990), p 150.
5 Answers will vary according to perception of importance and urgency. There are no correct answers, but possibles are: 1 Box I, 2 Box E, 3 Box B, 4 Box A, 5 Box F, 6 Box E, 7 Box D, 8 Box G, 9 Box H, 10 Box C.
6 Gordon MacDonald, 'Ideas That Work', *Leadership* (Summer 1987), pp 61, 62.
7 Tom Peters, *Thriving on Chaos* (Macmillan: London, 1988), and quoted in *The Sunday Times*, Section E Appointments (28 February 1988).
8 John Lubbock, *The Pleasures of Life* (Macmillan: London), and quoted in *Reader's Digest* (October 1990), p 77.
9 Thomas Weld, *Baptist Bulletin Service*, quoted in *Reader's Digest* (February 1991), p 107.

6: I DON'T HAVE TIME TO DO THAT NOW

1 'Why did they come to Leadership 89?' survey October 1989, pp 5, 14; jointly sponsored by the Evangelical Alliance and MARC Europe.

2 For example, *Leaders Under Pressure*, MARC Europe Research Monograph 37 (1991).

3 Robert Waterman, *The Renewal Factor* (Bantam Books, 1988), p 17.

4 *Ibid*, p 19.

5 *Leaders Under Pressure*, p 21.

6 Mary Holder Naegeli, 'Gently Arresting Time Bandits', *Leadership* (Fall 1989), p 126.

7 John Dawson, *Amarillo's Globe News*, quoted in *Reader's Digest* (January 1991), p 67.

8 I. Holmes, Stockport, *Reader's Digest* desk calendar and appointments book, 1990.

9 Walter A. Green and Harold Lazanes, 'Are you meeting with success?', *Executive Excellence* (October 1990), p 11.

10 Bryn Hughes, handout for 'Effective Use of Time' seminar, MARC Europe, 1989, pp 48, 49.

11 Sir John Hunt, 'Do's and Dont's of Chairmanship', *Management and Organisation* (July 1967).

12 Hughes, *op cit*, p 49.

13 'How Gender Specific is Ministry?', *Leadership* (Winter 1991), p 26.

14 Nancy Becker, 'Can Men and Women Work Together?', *Leadership* (Winter 1991), p 22.

15 Hunt, *op cit*.

16 John Townsend, 'How to Master Meetings', *Management Today* (July 1987), pp 81, 82.

17 Martyn Dunning and Lance Pierson, *Adminisheet 22* (August 1988), p 2.

18 Naegeli, *op cit*, p 123.

19 *Ibid*.

20 *Ibid*.

21 Hughes, *op cit*, p 47.

22 *Social Trends*, 1991 edition (Central Statistical Office, HMSO, 1990).

[23] Suzanne Wardall, 'Telephone Techniques', MARC Europe seminar, 1989.

[24] C.P. Miscavish, 'Towards More Picturesque Speech', *Reader's Digest* (June 1990), p 17.

[25] Jack D. Ferner, *Successful Time Management* (John Liley: Chichester, 1980), p 171.

[26] *Ibid*, p 177.

[27] *Ibid*, p 178.

[28] John Haggai, *Lead On!* (Word Book: Texas, USA, 1986), p 116.

[29] Job 3:25.

[30] 2 Timothy 1:7.

[31] Gordon MacDonald, 'Storing and Retrieving Sermon Material', *Leadership* (Winter 1987), pp 61, 62.

[32] Donald A. Laird and Eleanor C. Laird, *The Techniques of Delegating* (McGraw-Hill: London, 1957), p 3.

[33] Ted Engstrom, *The Making of a Christian Leader* (Zondervan: Michigan, USA), p 164; and quoted in Paul Beasley-Murray, *Dynamic Leadership* (MARC: Eastbourne, 1990), p 139.

[34] Laird, *op cit*, p 79.

[35] *Ibid*, p 14.

[36] *Ibid*, p 15.

[37] *Ibid*, pp 130–134.

[38] *Ibid*, pp 136–146.

[39] Edward R. Dayton, handout for 'Managing Your Time' seminar, MARC International, 1976, p 98.

[40] Laird, *op cit*, pp 176, 177.

[41] Dayton, *op cit*, pp 106–109, and used by permission of the publisher, the American Management Association.

[42] *Ibid*, p 103.

[43] Stephen R. Covey, 'An Inside-Out Approach', *Executive Excellence* (October 1990), p 3.

7: TIME TO STAND AND STARE—WHAT ME?

[1] Stephen Schofield, 'Three Gentlemen of the Press', *The Canadian C.S. Lewis Journal*, No 74 (Spring 1991), p 13.

2 Martyn Dunning and Lance Pierson, 'Did Jesus Keep a Filofax?', *Adminisheet 22*, August 1988.

3 John 21:25.

4 Dunning and Pierson, *op cit*.

5 Robert H. Schuller, *Your Church Has a Fantastic Future* (Regal Books, 1986).

6 C.S. Lewis, *The Screwtape Letters* (Collins: London, 1955), p 143.

7 'Fruits of Hope', *Christopher News Notes*, No 319.

8 C. Neil Strait, 'Tips on Time Management', *The Clergy Journal* (February 1990), p 21.

9 International Evangelical Lutheran Church in Helsinki, News, April 1989, p 2.

10 Peter W. Brierley, *'Christian' England* (MARC Europe, March 1991), p 212.

11 Genesis 18:14.

12 Luke 1:37.

13 Mark 9:23.

14 1 Corinthians 9:24.

APPENDICES

1 J. B. Middlebrook, *William Carey* (Carey Kingsgate Press, 1961), pp 64−65.

2 Donna Schaper, First Congregational Church, Riverhead, New York, *Leadership* (Spring 1991), pp 30 32.

INDEX

BRITISH CHURCH GROWTH ASSOCIATION

The British Church Growth Association was formed in September 1981 by a widely representative group of Christians committed to church growth either as researchers, teachers, practitioners or consultants. Following the Lausanne Congress on World Evangelisation in 1974, much interest was aroused in Church Growth thinking, which in turn led to the first UK Church Growth Consultation in 1978. Also during the 1970's a number of denominations had taken some church growth thinking and developed it within their own networks. A number of theological colleges and Bible colleges also began to teach church growth theory, particularly in their missionary departments. The Bible Society had begun to develop church growth courses that were being received enthusiastically. Developments in the work of the Evangelical Alliance led to the setting up of a Church Growth Unit and the publication of a *Church Growth Digest*. This unit drew together a number of leaders involved in the church growth field, but it was agreed to widen its impact by the formation of an association which would be even more comprehensive and effective.

Definition

Church Growth investigates the nature, function, structure, health and multiplication of Christian churches as they relate to the effective implementation of Christ's commission to 'Go then to all peoples everywhere and make them my disciples' (Matthew 28:19). Church Growth seeks to combine the revealed truths of the Bible with related insights from the contemporary social and behavioural sciences. Although not linked to any one school of church growth it owes much to the formational thinking of Dr Donald McGavran.

Aims

The BCGA aims to help and encourage the Church in Britain to move into growth in every dimension. The facilities and resources of the BCGA are available to researchers, consultants, teachers, practitioners and those just setting out in church growth thinking. The Association endeavours to offer practical help as well as encouraging and initiating Church Growth thinking and research.

Activities

The following are among its activities:

—Producing a quarterly journal particularly geared to the British scene with practical, biblical and theoretical articles of help to the churches as well as offering a forum for the sharing of views.
—Producing a number of occasional in-depth papers on a variety of topics.
—Co-publishing books on Church Growth.
—Running a specialist Church Growth book service offering discounted books to members and producing a catalogue of recommended church growth reading.
—Operating a reference system for information and personnel.
—Organising biennial residential conferences on particular topics of Church Growth relevant to the church in this country, eg Church Planting 1983, Conversion 1985, Bridge Building 1987. Various conferences have also been held in mainline Europe.
—Encouraging, co-ordinating or organising lectures and sem-

inars on particular subjects or with particular speakers which could be of help to the churches.
—Carrying out research in allied fields and building up a research register of work already done or being undertaken in various centres.
—Monitoring church growth at home and overseas.
—Linking in with a European initiative to share insights peculiar to the continent of Europe.
—Encouraging grass-roots involvement through seventeen regional groups.

Government

The Council of the BCGA is made up of 15 elected members and 7 co-opted members who meet 3 times a year. Although members serve in a personal capacity, the Council aims to be representative of geographical region, denomination and churchmanship, practitioner, researcher and teacher.

The day-to-day running of the Association is carried out by an officer with some secretarial assistance and the active support of members of the Council. The offices are situated in 3a Newnham Street, Bedford MK40 2JR and the telephone number is 0234-327905. The BCGA is a registered charity, no. 28557.

Membership

Membership of the BCGA is open to both individuals and organisations interested in or involved in the theory or practice of Church Growth. On payment of an annual subscription members are entitled to receive the *Church Growth Digest* (the journal of the Association) four times a year, information about activities through the Newsletters, special discounts on conferences and books, membership of the Church Growth Book Service, voting rights to elect members to the Council every two years, links with other researchers, teachers, practitioners, and consultants on a regional or national level as well as help or advice on allied matters.

The current subscription is £12.50 for individual membership and £25.00 for organisations or churches.

Further information about the Association and membership is available from the Secretary, British Church Growth Association, 3a Newnham Street, Bedford MK40 2JR.